CREATING
AUTISM CHAMPIONS

The resources and PowerPoint presentations that accompany this book can be downloaded at www.jkp.com/voucher using the code BEANEYAUTISM.

of related interest

Can I tell you about Autism?
A guide for friends, family and professionals
Jude Welton
Illustrated by Jane Telford
ISBN 978 1 84905 453 9
eISBN 978 0 85700 829 9

Is It OK to Ask Questions about Autism?
Abi Rawlins
Foreword by Michael Barton
ISBN 978 1 78592 170 4
eISBN 978 1 78450 439 7

Literacy for Visual Learners
Teaching Children with Learning Differences to Read, Write, Communicate and Create
Adele Devine
Illustrated by Quentin Devine
ISBN 978 1 84905 598 7
eISBN 978 1 78450 054 2

Flying Starts for Unique Children
Top Tips for Supporting Children with SEN or Autism When They Start School
Adele Devine
ISBN 978 1 78592 001 1
eISBN 978 1 78450 241 6

CREATING
AUTISM CHAMPIONS

AUTISM AWARENESS TRAINING FOR KEY STAGE 1 AND 2

JOY BEANEY

ILLUSTRATIONS BY HAITHAM AL-GHANI

Jessica Kingsley *Publishers*
London and Philadelphia

First published in 2017
by Jessica Kingsley Publishers
73 Collier Street
London N1 9BE, UK
and
400 Market Street, Suite 400
Philadelphia, PA 19106, USA

www.jkp.com

Library of Congress Cataloging in Publication Data
Title: Creating autism champions : autism awareness training for primary
    schools / Joy Beaney ; illustrations by Haitham Al-Ghani.
Description: Philadelphia : Jessica Kingsley Publishers, 2017. | Includes
    bibliographical references.
Identifiers: LCCN 2016046971 | ISBN 9781785921698 (alk. paper)
Subjects: LCSH: Autistic children--Education (Primary) | Autistic
    children--Education--Curricula.
Classification: LCC LC4717 .B4 2017 | DDC 371.94--dc23 LC record available at https://lccn.loc.
gov/2016046971

British Library Cataloguing in Publication Data
A CIP catalogue record for this book is available from the British Library

ISBN 978 1 78592 169 8
eISBN 978 1 78450 441 0

Printed and bound in Great Britain

The resources and PowerPoint presentations that accompany this book can be downloaded at www.jkp.com/voucher using the code BEANEYAUTISM.

CONTENTS

CONTENTS

ACKNOWLEDGEMENTS

I would like to thank the children, parents and professionals I have worked with throughout my career. I would particularly like to thank Kay Al-Ghani for her inspiration and encouragement and her son, Haitham, for the delightful illustrations he has drawn for this book.

INTRODUCTION

One of the best ways to help children with Autism feel accepted in school is by *increasing understanding of the condition amongst their peers and teachers.*

The National Autistic Society 2017a, para.4

Research indicates that the prevalence of Autism is about 1 child in 100 (Baird *et al.* 2006). In 1943 Leo Kanner, an Austrian paediatrician working in North America, published a paper entitled 'Early Infantile Autism'. His work described the case histories of children who had in common an unusual pattern of behaviour.

Everyone is unique, and Autism affects people in different ways. This is why it is often referred to as an Autism spectrum.

Some children in mainstream classes may have been given a diagnosis of Asperger Syndrome. The syndrome is named after Hans Asperger. Asperger was an Austrian paediatrician working at the same time as Leo Kanner. He identified a pattern of abilities and behaviours in a group of children who attended his clinic. He called them his 'Little Professors'. His work was not translated into English until the 1980s.

Hans Asperger had a very positive attitude towards those who have the syndrome and wrote:

> It seems that for success in science or art a dash of Autism is essential. For success the necessary ingredient may be an ability to turn from the everyday world, from the simply practical, an ability to rethink a subject with originality so as to create untrodden ways, with all abilities channelled into the one speciality. (Asperger 1979, cited in Attwood 2005, p.126)

In the DSM-5 diagnostic criteria published in 2013, a separate diagnosis of Asperger Syndrome is no longer given and it is included under the umbrella term 'Autistic spectrum' (American Psychiatric Association 2013).

It is recognised that children with Autism have many strengths, but they do have a different way of thinking and making sense of the world. This can often lead to difficulties in communicating and interacting with peers, as well as inflexible or rigid thinking. They may also have unusual responses to sensory stimuli.

Understanding the strengths and reasons why a pupil with Autism reacts as they do in a particular situation can offer a suitable approach to support the pupil.

One issue identified by the National Autistic Society (2017b) is that 'Autistic children and young people can be more at risk of being bullied than their peers because of the different ways they communicate and interact with others.'

Morewood, Humphrey and Symes (2011, p.66) proposed that 'much of the bullying, teasing and social exclusion that is often targeted at pupils with Autism is fuelled by ignorance'. Morewood explains that pupils observe children with Autism behaving differently, resulting in staff often treating them differently. Morewood believes that by giving an explanation and developing peer awareness, misunderstandings and resentment can be avoided.

Reid and Batten (2006, p.6) concur: 'Raising awareness of Autism among other children can help them understand why someone may act differently to them. It can encourage them to support children with Autism and discourage bullying among their peers.'

RATIONALE FOR THE DEVELOPMENT OF THE RESOURCE

A major part of my work advocating for children with Autism in mainstream schools has always been to implement practical strategies and approaches to reduce barriers to learning. However, whilst these strategies undoubtedly helped the children to cope with the day-to-day problems encountered, it became evident that when the children reached 8 or 9 years of age, new issues emerged surrounding the difficulties they had with social acceptance. It is a mistake to assume that because children with Autism lack intrinsic social skills, many do not want to socialise and have friends. A study by Ochs *et al.* (2001) suggests that it is their peers without Autism who hold the key to the successful inclusion for children with Autism and not the teachers. The children with Autism in the study showed they were able to understand and be distressed by being made the butt of jokes and by derisive behaviour from their classmates. Results indicated that classmates could effectively include or exclude children with Autism, depending upon whether they exhibited negative or positive responses. The same study pointed out that the children whose diagnosis was disclosed enjoyed more consistent social support, both in the classroom and on the playground.

Leading an outreach team supporting children with Autism in mainstream schools gave me the opportunity to analyse the social difficulties children with Autism were having and address the role played by the children's peers in successful inclusion. Taking into account the research by Ochs *et al.* (2001), I looked closely at the schools in which the Outreach Team was supporting children with Autism. It was obvious that awareness training for children without Autism, promoting acceptance and explaining ways to help children with Autism, was not taking place. Of course, all children were expected to behave in an inclusive way, but actual training of children in understanding Autism was sadly lacking. We tried to alter this situation by the Outreach Team going into schools and giving whole-school assemblies that highlighted the achievements of individuals with Autism. We felt it was important to give a positive message about Autism, describing the pupils' strengths but also explaining the differences and possible challenges the pupils might face. We invited classes to select children who would like to become the 'champions' of children with Autism. The children selected had good social skills. We then worked with groups of these children aged between 8 and 11 years and, meeting weekly, we devised lessons intended to increase their awareness and sensitivity towards children with Autism. We asked the children for their ideas on how to ensure that school was a fun and positive place to be for a child on the Autism spectrum. The children were awarded badges that they wore at playtimes so other pupils were able to identify them. Peers were able to help at transition times, break times and lunchtimes and staff reported that this helped to reduce the pupil with Autism's anxiety in these situations. Many of the schools we worked in had 'Friendship benches', so any child who sat there knew one of their peers would come and ask them to play or help them if they had difficulties understanding what was going on around them in the playground.

For many pupils with Autism, being amongst the other children on the playground can be an overwhelming experience. Sometimes the pupil with Autism may need a quiet place to go to be either alone or with a small number of peers. Many of the schools we worked in created lunchtime clubs that the pupil with Autism could access. This was particularly valuable when the club was based on the pupil with Autism's special interest, as they were able to show their strength and gain the respect and approval of their peers.

Children usually learn many of their social skills in an unconscious and intuitive way through observing and interacting with others, whereas children with Autism need to be taught explicitly. Many pupils with Autism will need a social skills intervention programme, but having learnt a social skill, playing and interacting with supportive peers gives opportunities to generalise the newly learnt skill.

Schools noticed positive outcomes following the peer awareness intervention. The pupils with Autism were observed to have more positive interactions with their peers, as the volunteers who completed the peer awareness training created a support network. The volunteers were more empathetic as they gained a greater understanding of the strengths and differences of the pupil with Autism.

Teaching peers about Autism can take place in a generalised way when it is not related to a particular pupil or it can be much more specific to the needs of a particular pupil. It is essential to work in partnership with the child and their parents. It is important to let parents know your plans for raising awareness of Autism. Explain why you feel the pupil will benefit and also the benefits to their peers.

It is a very sensitive issue, and some parents will not have told their child about their diagnosis. Even if the child is aware that they have Autism, parents may not wish this to be common knowledge. Parents have an invaluable insight into their child and may be able to provide useful information and strategies that they would like to be shared. The child's views must be respected and it is vital to discuss whether they wish to contribute to the assembly or lesson and what information about themselves they would like to be shared. Some children may prefer not to be present but would like staff to explain certain things about them, for example, why they react in a particular way, or to describe their sensory sensitivities. Sometimes the parents and the pupil have discussed what they would like others to know and have prepared a poster with drawings and written information that they wish to share. We have found that many children like to input into the assembly and that it has a very positive outcome.

Creating children who will be able to act as champions for children with Autism will set up a framework for the future, which is essential as the increasing numbers of children on the Autism spectrum will change to increasing numbers of adults with Autism in our community. If we start to educate all children, perhaps in years to come we can ensure that communities will look out for and care about them. Perhaps having Autism will come to be seen as a badge of honour, worthy of our respect and admiration.

USING THIS RESOURCE

Peer awareness

The resource includes a presentation for pupils, a ready-to-use assembly plan and lesson plans, with slides to support these. These can be accessed online from www.jkp.com/voucher using the code BEANEYAUTISM and downloaded for use. The presentation can be shown on the screen or the slides can be printed out for pupils to hold up. Within the book there are notes and photocopiable/downloadable resources to support the assembly. The accompanying notes should enable staff to deliver the assembly and lessons with confidence.

Using the peer awareness materials

The peer awareness materials can be used flexibly. We have used them successfully in different ways to fulfil the school's needs.

Two examples of ways the peer awareness materials have been used are given here.

- The assembly can stand alone and be delivered to the whole school to raise awareness of Autism and form part of the personal, social, health and economic (PSHE) education curriculum focusing on difference. The assembly could also be delivered to a class or small group and form the introductory lesson of the series. Staff can adapt the lessons to make them age appropriate to the children in their class and choose the elements that suit their setting.

- A short assembly about Autism can be delivered to the whole school. During that assembly you can ask for volunteers who would like to find out how to support their peers. The peer awareness materials can then be delivered as a series of lessons with this group of volunteers who are then able to be 'champions for Autism' and support their peers both in the classroom and playground. We found this was a particularly effective way to use the resource.

Staff training

The resource contains a ready-to-use training presentation, 'Autism in the Inclusive Classroom', which can be accessed online from www.jkp.com/voucher using the code BEANEYAUTISM and downloaded for use. Notes to accompany the training presentation are provided in the book.

PART 1

RAISING PEER AWARENESS

Assembly Notes and Lesson Plans

> The PowerPoint presentation for this part can be downloaded at www.jkp.com/voucher using the code BEANEYAUTISM.

PEER AWARENESS ASSEMBLY NOTES

Autism Awareness for the Whole School

PEER AWARENESS ASSEMBLY OR INTRODUCTORY LESSON PLAN

Lesson title: What is Autism?

Introduction

The ready-to-use assembly slides can be downloaded at www.jkp.com/voucher using the code BEANEYAUTISM and shown on the screen to pupils. If you would like the children to be more involved in delivering the assembly, slides could be printed out for the pupils to hold up. Notes are provided to enable staff to deliver the assembly with confidence.

If you do not wish to deliver this material as an assembly the information can form an introductory lesson about Autism for the class or a small group.

Learning objectives

- To introduce the term 'Autism'.
- To promote awareness and acceptance of pupils with Autism.
- To explain how pupils can help their peers with Autism.

Resources

- Laptop
- Projector
- Assembly PowerPoint slides (slides 1–19)
- Mozart CD

- Resource 1: A–U–T–I–S–M assembly cards – write how children can support their peers on the reverse of letters (the downloadable versions of the cards are enlarged to give one letter per page, so I'd suggest downloading and printing this resource rather than photocopying it)
- Arrange 6 chairs facing the audience

Teaching and learning activity

Introduction: Explain that the aim of the assembly is to raise awareness of Autism. Ask pupils to raise their hands if they have heard of Autism. Explain that 1 in 100 people have Autism.

Peer Awareness Assembly and Lesson Plans – Slide 2

Teacher's script: Autism affects how a person communicates and interacts with other people. It also affects how they make sense of the world around them. Having Autism means you have a different way of seeing the world that can sometimes makes it difficult to understand people. People are born with Autism – you cannot catch it from another person.

Peer Awareness Assembly and Lesson Plans – Slide 3

Teacher's script: Everyone is different and Autism affects people differently. Some people may have mild Autism and others have Autism that is more severe. Some children with Autism may be very smart. Some children with Autism don't seem to want to communicate with people and may not talk. Some children with Autism want friends but don't know how to make friends.

This is why it is called an Autism spectrum.

Peer Awareness Assembly and Lesson Plans – Slide 4

Teacher's script: In our school we may see children on the Autism spectrum.

People with Autism can find change difficult to cope with and get anxious if their routine changes. They may be very sensitive to things around them in their environment and, for example, might find sounds in the classroom or everyone playing in the playground too noisy for them. People with Autism have difficulty understanding other people's thoughts and feelings. Some people with Autism can find it difficult to express when they are feeling anxious, angry or frustrated in an appropriate way so may react aggressively.

Activity: Choose 6 children to come to the front of the assembly hall to hold up the large letters spelling 'AUTISM'.

Turn the cards over one by one to reveal how they can support a pupil with Autism and become a champion for Autism.

Peer Awareness Assembly and Lesson Plans – Slide 6

Teacher's script: We know that people with Autism have a different way of thinking and seeing the world.

We are all different and have different strengths and we all need help with some things.

Peer Awareness Assembly and Lesson Plans – Slide 8

Teacher's script: If we don't understand something we can get anxious and upset. By learning about Autism we can understand the person and help them.

Peer Awareness Assembly and Lesson Plans – Slide 10

Teacher's script: Teach others about Autism. Tell a friend, your parents or grandparents.

Peer Awareness Assembly and Lesson Plans – Slide 12

Teacher's script: Include children with Autism in what you do – say 'It is okay to be different – you are still one of us and we will look after you and help you.'

Peer Awareness Assembly and Lesson Plans – Slide 14

Teacher's script: Be kind and helpful. People with Autism can get very anxious – reassure them.

If things change they may get anxious, for example if the teacher is away or if the timetable changes.

Peer Awareness Assembly and Lesson Plans – Slide 16

Teacher's script: You can help if people with Autism want to be friends but don't know how. Including a person with Autism in your play can help them learn the rules for being a good friend.

Peer Awareness Assembly and Lesson Plans – Slide 18

We are learning to be Autism Champions

Peer Awareness Assembly and Lesson Plans – Slide 19

Some famous people are thought to have had Autism

A Statue of Mozart in London

Teacher's script: This is a statue of Mozart in London. Mozart was a gifted musician and composer. As a young child he performed to royalty and composed his own music. He is thought to have had Autism. We are going to end our assembly by listening to some music by Mozart.

Play music by Mozart to end the assembly.

PEER AWARENESS LESSON PLANS FOR AUTISM CHAMPIONS

INTRODUCTION

Lesson plans are provided which detail:

- Learning objectives

- Resources needed to deliver the lesson

- Teaching and learning activities, with comprehensive notes for each session to enable staff to deliver the lessons with confidence

- Suggested assessment criteria.

The ready-to-use slides can be downloaded at www.jkp.com/voucher using the code BEANEYAUTISM.

In the lessons two characters who have Autism, Sarah and Mike, explain their strengths and differences. They offer suggestions about how their classmates can support them.

Activities have been suggested for Key Stage 1 and Key Stage 2 children. Staff can choose those that are most appropriate for the children in their class. The lessons have been designed to be suitable to be delivered to a whole class or to a smaller group of children.

PEER AWARENESS LESSON PLAN 1

Lesson title: A different way of thinking

Learning objectives

- To understand that everyone is different.
- To know that we all have strengths but that we also need help with different things.
- To know that pupils with Autism think differently.

Resources

- Laptop
- Projector
- Lesson 1 PowerPoint slides (slides 20–27)
- Writing implements
- Resource 2: Lesson 1 quiz: How do you like to learn?
- Resource 3: Lesson 1: How do you learn best?

Teaching and learning activity

Introduction: Ask children what they can remember about the peer awareness assembly. Recap information about Autism.

Peer Awareness Assembly and Lesson Plans – Slide 21

Activity (Key Stages 1 and 2): Game – tell pupils to do the actions if they have the attribute or interest that you describe, for example, stand on one leg if you have brown hair, put your hands on your head if you like football, stand up if you have a brother, touch your toes if you are good at art.

Activity (Key Stage 2): Working in pairs, one pupil should pretend to be a newspaper reporter and ask questions about their peer's interests then swap roles.

Feed back what pupils found out about each other.

Emphasise that everyone is unique and has different skills and interests. Explain that a pupil with Autism often has a special interest and can be very knowledgeable about it. Explain that they may want to talk about it all the time and although it is good to share their interest they need help to widen their interests.

Peer Awareness Assembly and Lesson Plans – Slide 22

Explain that Sarah and Mike have Autism.

Teacher's script: Mike says: Hello, my name is Mike. I was born with Autism and it means my brain works in a different way to yours. I think differently. Let me try to explain. Look at this picture.

Peer Awareness Assembly and Lesson Plans – Slide 23

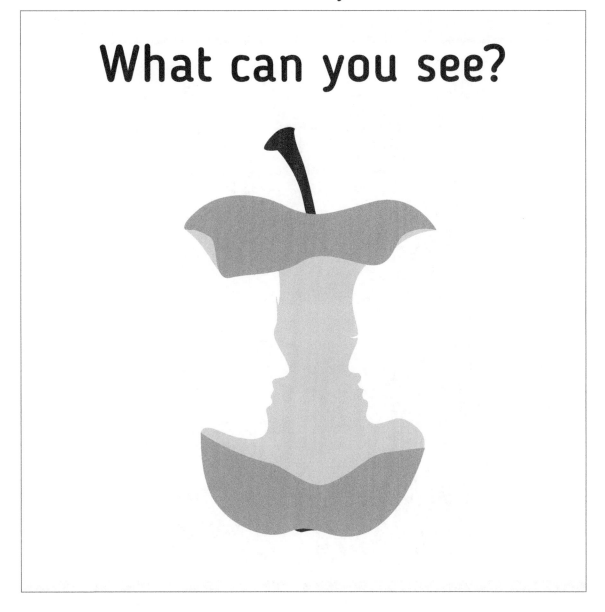

Teacher's script: Mike says: What can you see? I expect some of you saw the apple but others of you might have seen the 2 white heads.

Once you have seen the 2 images you will wonder why you couldn't see both of them in the first place!

Well, that is a bit like me. I sometimes don't understand things that everyone else seems to find easy. I need someone to teach me, then I know it. Then I think, why didn't I see that before?

You see we can all see the picture, but our brains can't always make sense of what we see. When this happens we need someone to help us understand.

I wish I had someone to help me see the things my brain can't seem to make sense of. Sometimes it feels like doing a jigsaw with pieces missing. Sometimes I don't get the full picture so I don't know how to behave.

Although I sometimes find it difficult to make sense of the whole situation, I am really good at focusing on detail.

Peer Awareness Assembly and Lesson Plans – Slide 24

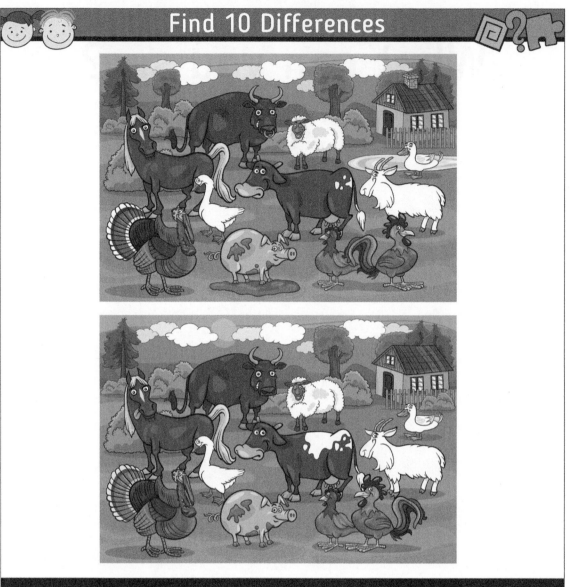

Ask if the pupils can find the differences in the images. The answers are given in the image on the next page.

Explain that children with Autism often develop particular skills.

· They can have an individual way of looking at the world – sometimes referred to as 'thinking outside the box'.

· They can be good at learning facts and skills when they are interested in them.

· They can concentrate for extended periods of time on an activity they are interested in and can become an expert in this.

Teacher's script: Mike says: It is hard having Autism because people can't see you have it. If I had a white stick you would know that I was blind and help me. If I had a wheelchair you would know I couldn't walk. If I had an inhaler you would know I had asthma, but with Autism people just think I am being difficult or naughty.

In the next few lessons I am going to tell you some other things I find difficult but also what I am really good at.

Peer Awareness Assembly and Lesson Plans – Slide 25

Activity (Key Stages 1 and 2): Complete 'Resource 2: Lesson 1 Quiz: How do you like to learn?' This will help pupils consider if they are a visual, auditory or kinaesthetic learner. Reiterate that everyone is unique and has different skills and interests, and we all need help sometimes to do things.

Peer Awareness Assembly and Lesson Plans – Slide 26

Think about what helps you to learn best.

I learn best when	I can look at a visual timetable	I work in a quiet place	I can use a plan or a visual map	I work in a clutter-free space
I have a checklist	I have a reward chart	I have time to think	I know how much time I have to complete a task	I am able to take a movement break
I work on my own	I work in a group	I work with a partner	I work with an adult	I can do my work on the computer

Alternative activity (Key Stage 2): Give out 'Resource 3: Lesson 1: How do you learn best?' Children should choose 5 things that help them learn, cut out the pictures and stick them on their worksheet.

Peer Awareness Assembly and Lesson Plans – Slide 27

Many children with autism are visual learners. Visual support can help them and lots of you too!

Example of a visual timetable

Timer

AUGUST						
Sun	Mon	Tues	Wed	Thurs	Fri	Sat
	1	2	3	4	5	6
7	8	9	10	11	12	13
14	15	16	17	18	19	20
21	22	23	24	25	26	27
28	29	30	31			

Calendar

I'm working for... Reward Chart

Explain that many people with Autism are visual learners and so using visual support can really help them.

Activity (Key Stages 1 and 2): Ask pupils to think of visual support they find helpful, for example, calendars, maps, symbols on toilet doors, traffic lights and a green man.

Plenary: Evaluate the session with the pupils, recap what has been taught and discuss the next session.

Assessment
Do pupils know:

- we all have strengths but we also all need help with different things?
- what helps them to learn best?

Evaluation of lesson

PEER AWARENESS LESSON PLAN 2

Lesson title: How we communicate

Learning objectives

- To understand what is meant by non-verbal language.
- To know in what ways non-verbal language is affected by Autism.
- To understand the communication difficulties a person with Autism may have.

Resources

- Laptop
- Projector
- Lesson 2 PowerPoint slides (slides 28–43)
- Resource 4: Lesson 2: Cards for non-verbal actions (or display using slides 30–37)
- Resource 5: Lesson 2: 'Oh' resource
- Resource 6: Lesson 2: Idiom cards

Teaching and learning activity

Introduction: Explain that today we are going to think about how we communicate with each others.

Activity (Key Stages 1 and 2): Ask pupils to find a partner and sit back to back. Ask them to have a conversation without looking at each other.

Teacher's script: How did this make you feel? Did you find it hard to carry on with the conversation if you couldn't see the other person's face? Could you tell if the other person was interested in what you had to say?

Explain that we use a lot of gesture and body language when we communicate with others.

Peer Awareness Assembly and Lesson Plans – Slide 29

Explain that many pupils with Autism may have difficulty understanding body language. Talk about the terms verbal and non-verbal language.

Explain that a lot of what we say does not use words, for example for 'I'm happy' we smile, for 'I don't know' we shrug our shoulders

Activity (Key Stages 1 and 2): Use 'Resource 4: Lesson 2: Cards for non-verbal actions'. Either do the activity with the whole group or ask a volunteer to choose a card with an instruction written on it and demonstrate the body language to illustrate it. The rest of class can guess what the non-verbal body language is showing.

Examples:

- Show me you are worried (for example, biting lips).
- Show me you are bored (look up and yawn).
- Using just your hands, show me you are angry (clenched fist).
- Show me you are confident and in control (hands on hips).
- Show me you are paying attention (sit up straight and look into the person's eyes).
- Ask me to be very quiet (finger on lips, hunch shoulders).
- Attract my attention to something without speaking (beckon, point, wave arms).
- Show me you are joking (wink).

Explain that we also show our feelings in the way we say a word with our tone of voice.

Activity (Key Stage 2): Show 'Resource 5: Lesson 2: "Oh" resource'. Ask children to say the word as if they are feeling the following:

- happy
- sad
- excited
- angry
- bored.

Teacher's script: Children with Autism often find it difficult to pick up how people are feeling through their tone of voice. This can lead to misunderstandings, as they might not realise you are angry or sad about something.

Peer Awareness Assembly and Lesson Plans – Slide 38

Show Mike's example of his difficulty understanding sarcasm: 'That's great!' meaning 'That's awful.'

Teacher's script: Mike says: I can't tell when someone is being sarcastic. For example, the other night when we had my favourite food – spicy pasta – I filled my bowl really, really full. My dad saw me and said, 'Do you think you have enough there?' I replied, 'I think so,' and everyone started laughing. He was being sarcastic. Then there was the time I asked my brother if I could have his old iPad and he said, 'Yeah right, on yer bike.' So I thought he meant he would leave it by my bike. Of course, what he meant was 'No, you can't!'

Explain that we know what the person means because we look at their body language and listen to their tone of voice to interpret what they mean.

Peer Awareness Assembly and Lesson Plans – Slide 39

Ask pupils to guess what the sayings on the following slides mean.

We get on like a house on fire

What does this saying mean?

Peer Awareness Assembly and Lesson Plans – Slide 41

I'm all ears

What does this saying mean?

Peer Awareness Assembly and Lesson Plans – Slide 42

I'm under the weather

What does this saying mean?

Peer Awareness Assembly and Lesson Plans – Slide 43

Explain the importance of speaking clearly and saying what you mean.

Explain that the pupil with Autism often doesn't understand when someone is joking.

Discuss how this could mean that the person with Autism could be taken advantage of.

Activity (Key Stage 2): Using 'Resource 6: Lesson 2: Idiom cards', and working in groups, give each child a saying to illustrate. Ask other children in the group to work out the meaning.

Plenary: Evaluate the session with the pupils, recap learning and discuss the next session.

Assessment
Do pupils understand:
   · what is meant by non-verbal language?
   · the communication difficulties a person with Autism may have?

Evaluation of lesson

PEER AWARENESS LESSON PLAN 3

Lesson title: Sensory differences

Learning objectives

- To know some possible sensory differences encountered by pupils with Autism.
- To understand that pupils with Autism may be anxious.

Resources

- Paper
- Red, green, blue and black crayons for each child
- Pencils with different textures
- Texture boxes
- Sand pots containing paperclips
- Rubber gloves
- Food items that are sweet, sour, bitter and salty
- Lesson 3 PowerPoint slides (slides 45–55)
- Resource 7: Lesson 3: Sensory simulation listening activity
- Resource 8: Lesson 3: Taste bud experiment
- Resource 9: Lesson 3: Glasses for sensory simulation – using peripheral vision
- Resource 10: Lesson 3: How might sensory differences affect your classmate?

Teaching and learning activity

Introduction: Explain that in today's session we are going to think about how we use our senses. Explain that we find out about the world through our senses. Ask pupils, 'What are our senses?'

Peer Awareness Assembly and Lesson Plans – Slide 45

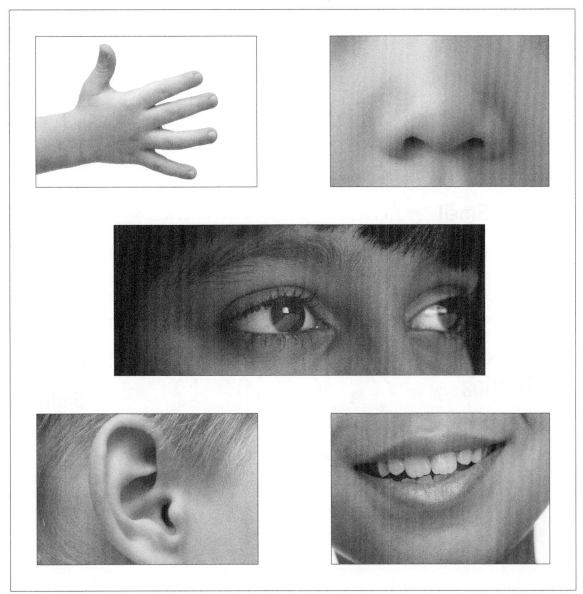

Teacher's script: Our senses take in information from our surroundings. Special cells send messages to the brain. The brain is constantly receiving and processing this information from our senses, which helps us understand what is going on around us and tells us how to respond.

We find out about the world through our senses of:

- **Touch**: Special cells in the skin enable us to feel textures, cold, heat and pain. Some parts of our skin are more sensitive than others.
- **Hearing**: Special cells in the inner ear enable us to hear sounds in the environment.
- **Sight**: Special cells at the back of the eyes enable us to identify objects, colours and 3D images.
- **Smell**: Special cells in the nose enable us to detect different smells.
- **Taste**: Our sense of taste comes from taste buds in our tongue. They enable us to distinguish between sweet, sour, bitter and salty.

Peer Awareness Assembly and Lesson Plans – Slide 46

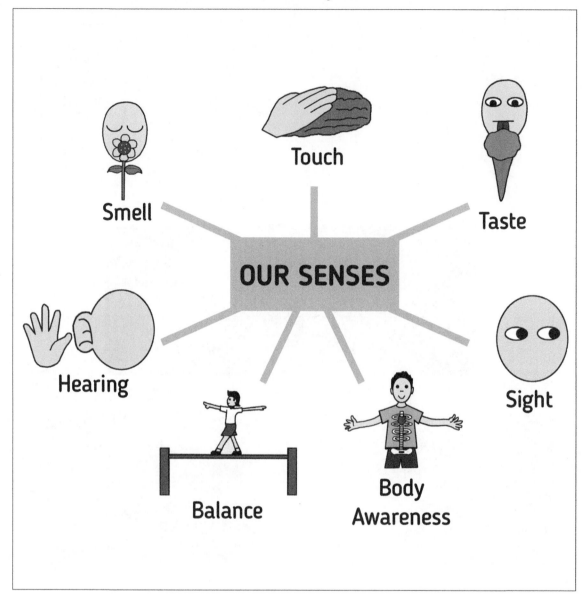

Teacher's script: There are 2 other sensory systems that are also important for our development.

- The balance system gives us information on balance and where our body is in space.
- The body awareness system enables us to know where our body parts are and how they are moving. It also helps us to know things such as whether we are hot, cold or hungry.

Talk about how Autism may affect a person's senses and give some examples.

Teacher's script: Many children with Autism may be overly sensitive to certain sensations or have low sensitivity where the brain doesn't get enough information about the situation or environment.

Explain that pupils with Autism may be very sensitive to certain sensory stimuli.

Peer Awareness Assembly and Lesson Plans – Slide 47

TOUCH

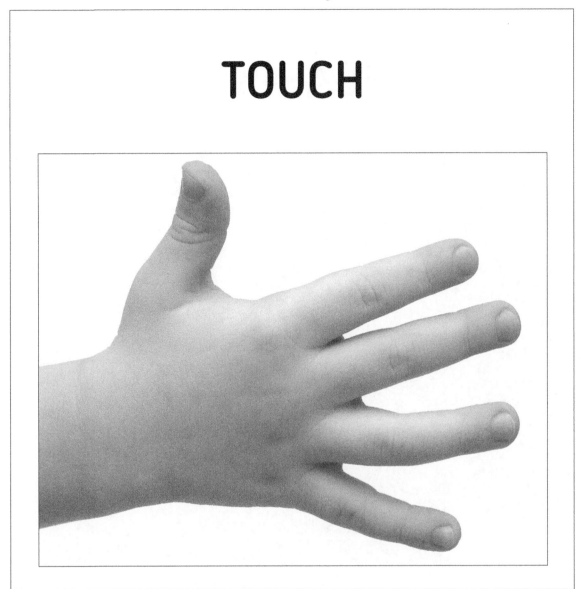

Sensitivity with touch can result in the child disliking things on their hands and therefore they may not want to do some practical activities. They may not like certain textures of clothes and find touch painful. If they have low sensitivity they may want to continually touch objects and people.

Peer Awareness Assembly and Lesson Plans – Slide 48

HEARING

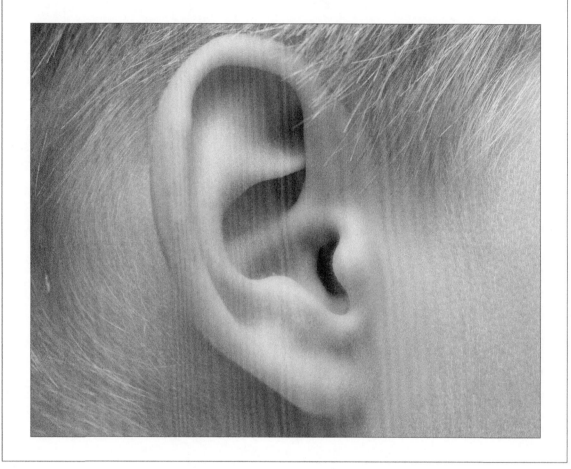

Sensitivity with hearing can result in the child finding the noise in a busy classroom or playground very difficult to cope with.

Peer Awareness Assembly and Lesson Plans – Slide 49

Peer Awareness Assembly and Lesson Plans – Slide 50

SIGHT

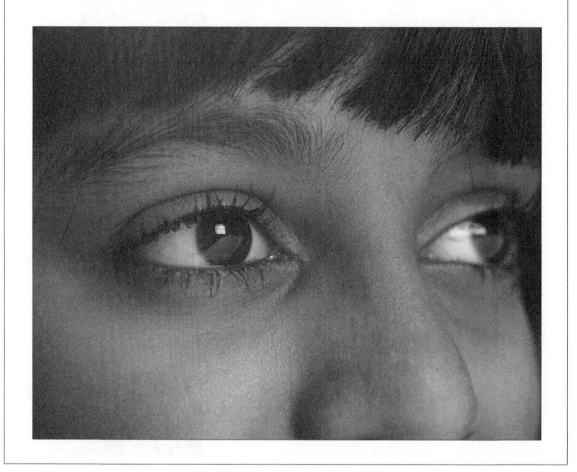

Sensitivity with sight can result in the child being sensitive to sunlight and electric lights.

Peer Awareness Assembly and Lesson Plans – Slide 51

SMELL

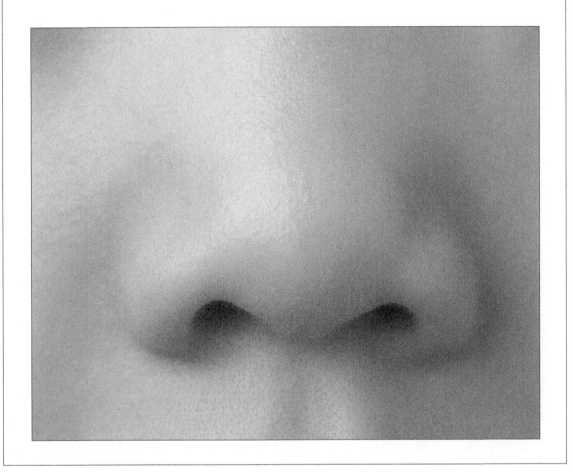

Sensitivity with smell can result in the child finding smells overpowering, and they may dislike the cooking smells coming from the school dining room or the smell of soaps and perfumes.

Peer Awareness Assembly and Lesson Plans – Slide 52

TASTE

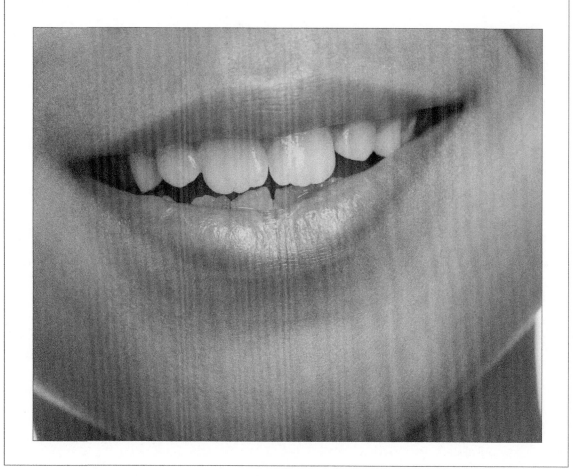

Sensitivity with taste can result in the child eating a limited range of food.

Peer Awareness Assembly and Lesson Plans – Slide 53

Sensitivity in the vestibular sense can result in the child being frightened of going on the PE apparatus.

Peer Awareness Assembly and Lesson Plans – Slide 54

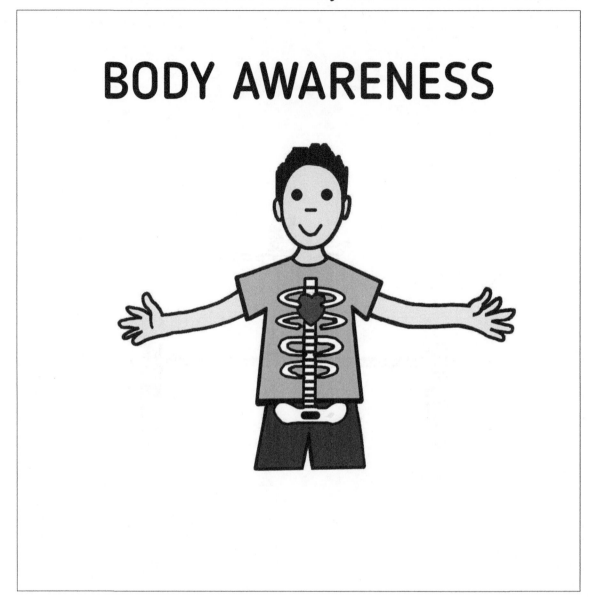

Sensitivity in the proprioceptive sense can result in the child having difficulty with activities that need good coordination. If they have low sensitivity they may not realise they are getting too hot or cold.

Sensory difficulties can lead to sensory overload, resulting in people being unable to cope in particular situations.

Show a sensory overload film – search for 'sensory overload autism' on YouTube, or the National Autistic Society has produced some film clips that can be found at www.autism.org.uk.

Explain that the pupils are going to do some activities to give them an idea of what it feels like when our senses are not working properly.

Teacher's script: This activity illustrates our difficulty in filtering out sounds, which affects our ability to concentrate on what the teacher is saying when others are talking.

Activity (Key Stage 2): Follow the instructions on 'Resource 7: Lesson 3: Sensory simulation listening activity'. After the activity, the children's drawings should look like the image on the resource.

Activity (Key Stages 1 and 2): Set up some of the following table-top activities. Pupils can complete the activity on their table and then move around to the next one.

- **Textured pencils activity:** Wrap strips of different textures around pencils and ask the pupils to try writing with them. Examples of textures include a strip of soft Velcro, a strip of rough Velcro, sandpaper and sticky tape with the sticky side outwards. This activity helps to illustrate that some people do not like touching particular textures and this could affect the way they do an activity.

- **Texture boxes activity:** Put a different object in each box and cover them with plastic bags so the children have to feel the object but cannot see it. Examples of textures/objects include a soft fluffy toy, a fir cone, sandpaper and gooey dough. This activity helps to illustrate a reluctance to touch objects when you know you are sensitive to textures.

- **Paperclip in the sand activity:** Hide some paperclips in small container of sand. Pupils should try to pick them out of the containers whilst wearing gloves. This activity helps to illustrate the difficulty in picking up an object if you are under-sensitive to texture.

- **Taste activity:** Provide foods with strong tastes for children to try, for example marmite, a sherbet sweet, sweet and salty popcorn, flavoured crisps and lemon. Pupils should record the savoury, sweet and bitter tastes on the tongue on 'Resource 8: Lesson 3: Taste bud experiment'. This activity helps to illustrate that we all have different likes and dislikes.

- **Smelling pots activity:** Fill containers with items that smell different, for example herbs, soaps and cotton wool with perfume on it. Cover and number the pots. Ask children to smell the numbered pots and try to identify what is in them. This activity helps to illustrate that we all have different likes and dislikes.

- **Looking sideways activity:** Make up the glasses with the centre of their lenses covered from 'Resource 9: Lesson 3: Glasses for sensory simulation - using peripheral vision'. Ask pupils to try talking to a friend whilst wearing the glasses. This helps to illustrate what it is like when you do not give eye contact. Explain that many people with Autism find it difficult to do this and use peripheral vision, which means looking out of the side of their eyes.

Activity (Key Stages 1 and 2): Complete the worksheet on 'Resource 10: Lesson 3: How might sensory differences affect your classmate?'

Peer Awareness Assembly and Lesson Plans – Slide 55

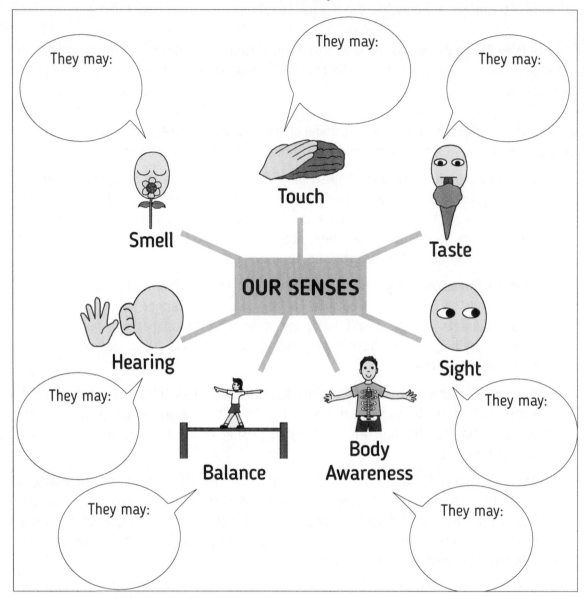

Plenary: Evaluate the session with the pupils, recap learning and discuss the next session.

Assessment
Do pupils understand:

· some possible sensory differences encountered by pupils with Autism?

Evaluation of lesson

PEER AWARENESS LESSON PLAN 4

Lesson title: Understanding our feelings

Learning objectives

- To recognise and name feelings.

- To know it is okay to have any feeling but not okay to behave in any way that hurts other people.

Resources

- Laptop
- Projector
- Lesson 4 PowerPoint slides (slides 56–57)
- Teddy bear
- Box
- Scrapbook
- Crayons, felt tips
- Pictures/catalogues/photos
- Glue sticks
- Resource 11: Lesson 4: Feelings circle
- Resource 12: Lesson 4: Worry symbol and cards

Teaching and learning activity

Introduction: Explain that today we are going to think about our feelings.

Peer Awareness Assembly and Lesson Plans – Slide 57

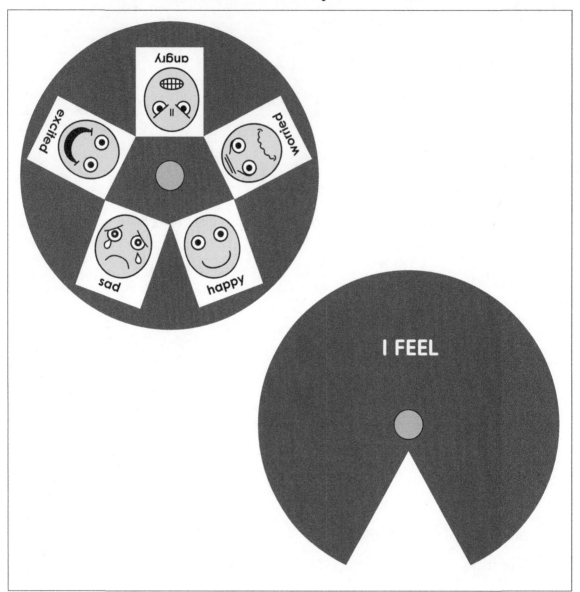

Activity (Key Stage 1): Play 'Bear Hugs' at circle time by passing a teddy bear around the group. Each child should give him a hug to make him happy. Ask pupils to show a happy face.

Give out 'Resource 11: Lesson 4: Feelings circle' and ask the pupils to find the happy picture on their 'feelings circle'.

Pupils should say: 'I feel happy when...' and then repeat this for the other feelings.

Sing the song 'If you are happy and you know it, clap your hands' and change the words for other verses to match the emotions:

- If you are sad and you know it say 'Boo hoo'.
- If you are excited and you know it jump up and down.
- If you are worried and you know it tell a friend.
- If you are angry and you know it count to 10.

Explain that pupils with Autism are often very anxious and this could result in them being unable to cope and possibly withdrawing, running away or becoming angry.

Activity (Key Stage 2): Use 'Resource 12: Lesson 4: Worry symbol and cards' to make a class worry box with the large 'worry' image on it. Ask pupils to write what worries them on small cards and post them in the box. Discuss with the class what has been written and how they can help each other to overcome their worries.

Ask pupils what makes them angry.

Ask pupils what helps them to be calm, and then introduce some calming activities.

- Count to 10 whilst breathing slowly.
- Walk away and go to a safe space.
- Think of a birthday cake. Take a deep breath and pretend to blow out the candles one at a time.
- Hug a soft toy, squeezing very hard.
- Go for a walk.
- Pretend to blow up a balloon, spread out your arms as it gets bigger and bigger.
- Put your hands together and push, and then relax and repeat.
- Place your hands against the wall and push hard, and then relax and repeat.
- Listen to calming music.
- Squeeze a squishy ball.
- Have a drink through a straw.

Ask the pupil to identify other things they think will help them to calm down.

Activity (Key Stages 1 and 2): Make a 'happy book'. Ask pupils to draw and stick in images of people and things they like. Ask them bring photos from home of things that are special to them, such as their family, pets, holidays or toys. Explain that when the pupil is feeling worried or angry they can look at their book and this will help them to calm down.

Plenary: Evaluate the session with the pupils, recap learning and discuss the next session.

Assessment
Do pupils understand that:

- it is okay to have any feeling but not okay to behave in any way that hurts other people?

Evaluation of lesson

PEER AWARENESS LESSON PLAN 5

Lesson title: Being a good friend

Learning objective

- To know how to be a good friend.

Resources

- Laptop
- Projector
- Lesson 5 PowerPoint slides (slides 58–61)

Teaching and learning activity

Introduction: Explain that today we are going to think about how we can be a good friend.

Explain that social skills are complex and take a long time for us to learn. Pupils with Autism often want to be social but sometimes don't know how to make friends

Peer Awareness Assembly and Lesson Plans – Slide 59

How to be a good friend

- A pupil with Autism may want to join in your play but not know how to ask – ask them to play.

- Explain situations or rules of the game. Remember they may not understand facial expressions or body language. They may also have difficulty understanding what other people are thinking or feeling – using drawings or visuals can help them to understand.

- Pupils with Autism do not like change, so help them in new situations and with changing from one activity to another.

Peer Awareness Assembly and Lesson Plans – Slide 60

How to be a good friend

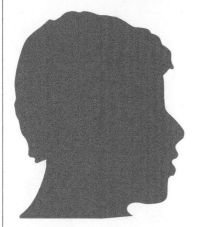
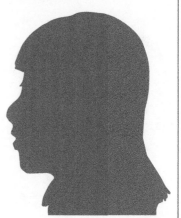

- Sometimes the pupil with Autism doesn't appear to take any notice of what you are saying, but it doesn't mean they are not interested – it just takes them longer to respond. Be patient.

- Speak clearly and say what you mean.

- Pupils with Autism may find it difficult to cope in some situations because of their sensory difficulties.

- Look out for your friend and help them if someone is teasing or bullying them.

Have fun together

Children with Autism may not understand the motives of their peers or may not understand unwritten social skills and this can mean they are very vulnerable and might be bullied. Discuss how the pupils can help others and what they should do if they think someone is being bullied.

Peer Awareness Assembly and Lesson Plans – Slide 61

Special Interests

Activity (Key Stages 1 and 2): Discuss ways we can share each others' interests. Many pupils with Autism are talented and very knowledgeable about their interest. Taking part in these activities could raise the pupil with Autism's self-esteem and earn them the respect of their peers. Ask pupils to think about activities they could do at a lunchtime club.

Plenary: Evaluate the session with the pupils, recap learning and discuss the next session.

Assessment
Do pupils understand:

· some ways to be a good friend?

Evaluation of lesson

PEER AWARENESS LESSON PLAN 6

Lesson title: Being an Autism Champion

Learning objectives

- To know ways to support a pupil with Autism.
- To accept difference.

Resources

- Laptop
- Projector
- Lesson 6 PowerPoint slides (slides 62–66)
- Writing implements
- Resource 13: Lesson 6: Autism Champion

Teaching and learning activity

Introduction: Today we are going to think about how we can support a pupil with Autism in our school.

Peer Awareness Assembly and Lesson Plans – Slide 63

ABOUT ME	Strengths and interests	Things I find difficult
	I like playing chasing and football in the playground.	Sometimes I get angry when we have to stop our game and come back into class.
	I am very good at remembering facts and I know a lot about space travel.	I don't understand why people are not interested when I tell them all the facts I know.
	Maths and Science are my favourite subjects.	I get upset when people change the timetable.
	I have got lots of joke books and I like reading them.	I often don't know when other people are joking.

What is Mike good at?
How might he need you to help him?

This slide shows Mike's profile with his strengths and differences. Ask pupils to say what his strengths are and what things he might need help with.

Peer Awareness Assembly and Lesson Plans – Slide 64

ABOUT ME	Strengths and interests	Things I find difficult
	I am very good at reading and spelling.	Sometimes I get confused if it is noisy in the classroom and can't understand what to do.
	I like talking to my friend at playtime.	I don't like playing games with lots of people and sometimes I get anxious and need to be on my own.
	I Love dancing and PE.	I find it difficult to sit still in class.
	I love drawing and like to do detailed drawings.	I like to do things perfectly and can get upset if I am not happy with my work.

What is Sarah good at?
How might she need you to help her?

This slide shows Sarah's profile with her strengths and differences. Ask pupils to say what her strengths are and what things she might need help with.

Peer Awareness Assembly and Lesson Plans – Slide 65

How can you support a classmate with Autism?

To cope with change

At playtime

To understand
what people say

To make friends

Activity (Key Stages 1 and 2): Give out 'Resource 13: Lesson 6: Autism Champion'. Children should come up with different ideas for supporting a pupil with Autism and share the ideas with the class or group.

Peer Awareness Assembly and Lesson Plans – Slide 66

Plenary: Evaluate the session with the pupils and recap learning.

Assessment

Do pupils understand:

- some ways to help a pupil with Autism?

Evaluation of the course

PART 2

SCHOOL STAFF NOTES FOR AUTISM AWARENESS TRAINING

The PowerPoint presentation from this part can be downloaded at www.jkp.com/voucher using the code BEANEYAUTISM.

AUTISM IN THE INCLUSIVE CLASSROOM

Training is an essential element in successfully supporting pupils with Autism. Consistency is key to successful inclusion and it is therefore important to raise the awareness of everyone on the staff team. This training could be delivered in one go or divided into the following shorter sessions:

- Understanding autism

- Supporting communication

- Supporting social skills

- A different way of thinking

- Sensory differences

- Supporting behaviour.

The notes on each slide can be used to support the trainer delivering the session.

UNDERSTANDING AUTISM

The National Autistic Society describes Autism as affecting:

how a person communicates with, and relates to, other people. It also affects how they make sense of the world around them. (National Autistic Society 2017b)

In Autism, effective teaching can only be realised by an initial consideration of the individual's way of learning and its effects on whatever the teacher might plan to do. Education in Autism needs to be pursued from the child's perspective. (Powell 2000, p.148)

This training will explain the strengths and differences experienced by the pupil with Autism. It will explain how, by making just a few accommodations, you can make your school fully inclusive.

An assembly and lesson plans for pupils have also been developed, as it is vital for a school to raise pupils' awareness if it is going to be considered to be inclusive.

Morewood, Humphrey and Symes (2011) proposed that misunderstandings and resentment can be avoided by giving an explanation and developing peer awareness.

CODE OF PRACTICE

Our vision for children with special educational needs and disabilities is the same as for all children and young people – that they achieve well in their early years, at school and in college, and lead happy and fulfilled lives. (SEND Code of Practice 2015, Foreword)

Lessons should be planned to address potential areas of difficulty and to remove barriers to pupil achievement. (SEND Code of Practice 2015, 6.12, p.94)

The SEND Code of Practice (Department for Education and Department of Health 2015) requires schools to make 'reasonable adjustments' to prevent children being at a disadvantage. It also states, 'Schools also have wider duties to prevent discrimination, to promote equality of opportunity and to foster good relations' (Department for Education and Department of Health 2015, p.93).

Books and articles written by people with Autism (for example, Grandin 2006; Lawson 2001) are helping us to gain a greater understanding. Trying to see the world through the eyes of the person with Autism can help everybody to think about how they can support the individual and make a difference.

Strategies that help the child with Autism will be of value to every child in the classroom.

PREVALENCE OF AUTISM IN UK

Around 700,000 people may have Autism, or more than 1 in 100 in the population. (National Autistic Society 2017b)

There is no central register of people with Autism. The figure of 1 in 100 is an estimate of the children in the UK with Autism taken from a survey by the Office of National Statistics and a survey in the South Thames area. Many people consider the prevalence of Autism to be higher than this. There are more boys than girls diagnosed with Autism (Charman *et al*. 2011). It is thought that many females are undiagnosed, which could partly be due to the diagnostic criteria focusing on male behaviour and traits. Girls with Autism present differently, often being shy or passive, having an increased ability to copy the behaviour of their peers to fit in and their intense interests focusing on similar things to other girls.

With the number of people receiving an Autism diagnosis, it is vital to increase understanding of Autism in both education and the wider community.

IMPACT OF AUTISM

strengths   differences

Children with Autism are often described in terms of their difficulties. It is important to remember that everyone has strengths. Just think how you would react if when applying for a job only your weaknesses and difficulties were described!

There are particular strengths and skills that children with Autism are likely to develop.

- They have an individual way of looking at the world, sometimes referred to as 'thinking outside the box'.

- They are good at learning facts and skills when they are interested in them.

- They are able to concentrate for extended periods of time on an activity they are interested in and can become an expert in this.

- They are able to focus on detail.

Staff Training – Slide 6

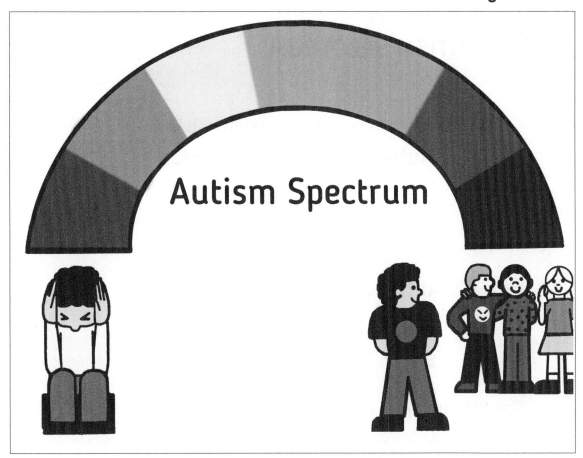

In 1943 Leo Kanner, an Austrian paediatrician working in North America, published a paper entitled 'Early Infantile Autism'. His work described the case histories of children who had in common an unusual pattern of behaviour.

Everyone is unique, and Autism affects people in different ways. This is why it is often referred to as an Autistic spectrum.

Autism can affect anyone, regardless of their intelligence. Some pupils may have learning difficulties or some may be non-verbal and prefer to be on their own, whereas at the other end of the spectrum the individual could be academically gifted but still have problems with social interaction and communication.

THE AUTISM SPECTRUM

Sometimes Autism is referred to as
Autistic Spectrum Disorder.

This is commonly abbreviated to
ASD.
Or it is referred to as
Autistic Spectrum Condition.

This is commonly abbreviated to
ASC.

Some children may have a diagnosis of Asperger Syndrome.

Sometimes Autism is referred to as an Autistic Spectrum Disorder or ASD. Many people with High Functioning Autism or Asperger Syndrome have said they do not consider themselves disordered but have a different way of thinking and prefer to call it an Autistic Spectrum Condition or ASC.

The language we use to talk about Autism can affect attitudes.

Staff Training – Slide 8

DIAGNOSIS

- **ICD-10** World Health Organisation's criteria for childhood Autism *International Classification of Diseases* (1992)

- **DSM-5** American Psychiatric Association's *Diagnostic and Statistical Manual of Mental Disorders* (2013)

There are 2 main diagnostic classifications: the ICD-10 (WHO 1992) and the DSM-5 (APA 2013).

You can't recognise someone with Autism from their appearance and there is no medical test to determine if a child has Autism. To get a diagnosis of Autism, information about the child's communication skills, how they relate to others, their emotional development and their cognitive skills are gathered. A diagnosis of Autism is often given by a paediatrician or multidisciplinary team following interactions with the child, observation of the child in different situations and discussions with parents/carers and family members. If the child is attending a nursery or school, the staff may be requested to provide a report on how the child is functioning in the school environment.

FEATURES OF AUTISM

In the ICD-10 the criteria for a diagnosis are difficulties in the following areas:

> **Social communication:**
> verbal and non-verbal.

> **Social interaction:**
> making and maintaining friendships.

> **Repetitive and restricted patterns of behaviour, interests and activities:**
> preoccupation with parts of an object, a dislike of change.

- **Social communication**: Difficulty understanding both verbal and non-verbal communication, for example, gesture, facial expression, body language and tone of voice. The pupil may take things literally and have difficulty understanding jokes and sarcasm.

- **Social interaction**: Difficulty understanding social rules. The pupil may find some social situations difficult to cope with and become very anxious.

- **Restricted range of interests, patterns of behaviour and activities**: Play is often repetitive and the child may have difficulty developing imaginative play. They may become distressed over small changes in routines or the environment. Many pupils with Autism find the world very unpredictable and find comfort in setting up routines they can control.

Staff Training – Slide 10

HANS ASPERGER

Hans Asperger had a very positive attitude towards those who have the syndrome, and wrote:

> It seems that for success in science or art a dash of Autism is essential. For success the necessary ingredient may be an ability to turn from the everyday world, from the simply practical, an ability to rethink a subject with originality so as to create untrodden ways, with all abilities channelled into the one speciality. (Asperger 1979, cited in Attwood 2005, p.126)

Some pupils in mainstream schools may have a diagnosis of Asperger Syndrome. The syndrome is named after Hans Asperger. Asperger was an Austrian paediatrician working at the same time as Leo Kanner. He identified a pattern of abilities and behaviours in a group of children who attended his clinic. He called them his 'Little Professors'. His work was not translated into English until the 1980s. Pupils with a diagnosis of Asperger Syndrome are considered to be on the Autism spectrum. These pupils are often of average or above average intelligence. Children with Asperger Syndrome often want friends but they may lack the social skills that are intuitive for us and this makes social interaction difficult and stressful.

DSM-5

In the DSM-5 the criteria for a diagnosis are difficulties in the following 2 areas:

- Social communication and interaction.

- Restricted, repetitive patterns of behaviour, interests or activities. Sensory difficulties are included in the criteria for the first time.

The DSM-5, produced by the American Psychiatric Society and published in 2013, emphasises the importance of identifying how much Autism affects the child and how much support they require. Sensory difficulties are included in the DSM-5 diagnostic criteria. A separate diagnosis of Asperger Syndrome is no longer given in this criteria and is included under the umbrella term 'Autistic spectrum'.

Staff Training – Slide 12

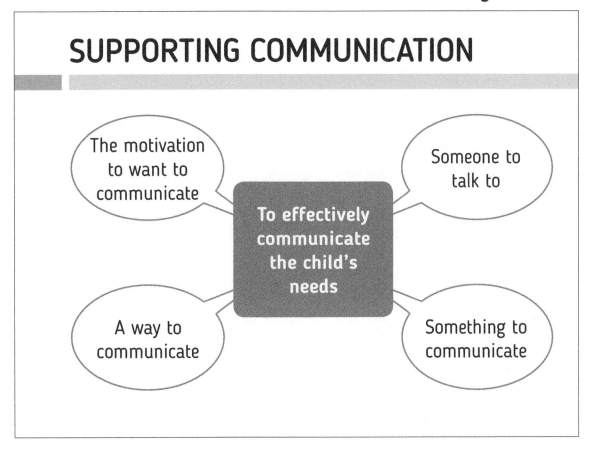

SUPPORTING COMMUNICATION

The motivation to want to communicate

Someone to talk to

To effectively communicate the child's needs

A way to communicate

Something to communicate

Communication is about both expressing oneself and understanding language. The child with Autism may have difficulty with both verbal and non-verbal communication.

Some children with Autism don't realise they can have an impact on their world and the people in it and may not develop speech. Others may use lots of language. It is important to recognise that an excellent verbal ability does not always mean that the child has a good understanding of what people are saying. The opposite is also true. People who are non-verbal may understand more than you think. The child may have difficulty understanding gesture and tone of voice.

The child may need to use visuals to support their communication.

IDEAS TO SUPPORT COMMUNICATION

- **Create as many communication opportunities as possible.**

- **Teach communication skills**, e.g. asking for help, asking for a break from an activity.

- **Use visual support to make your communication clearer.**

Speech may be repetitive and the child may often repeat what others have said. They may constantly ask questions and want the same reply. They may not recognise if the listener is interested and continue to talk about their special interest. They may make tactless remarks or make comments out of context. Pupils with Autism often have difficulty understanding abstract concepts such as time.

Create as many meaningful opportunities as possible for the child to communicate during the school day. Identify the child's interests, as this can be a way to engage the child in communication and develop their skills.

Role play and modelling of language can be good ways to develop skills.

Staff Training – Slide 14

THINK ABOUT THE WAY YOU COMMUNICATE

- **To get the child's attention, say their name before an instruction.**

- **Wait and give the child time to process an instruction.**

- **Give an instruction in the order you want the child to do it**, e.g. change 'We can't go to the playground until you have put your shoes on' to 'Shoes on, then we can go to the playground'.

- **Use positive language** – avoid 'no' and 'don't'.

- **Say what you want the child to do** rather than what you don't want to happen, e.g. change 'Don't run' to 'Walk'.

If an instruction is given to the whole class, the pupil with Autism may not realise that it applies to them so it is important to say their name to ensure you have their attention.

It is a good idea to count to 10 before repeating an instruction to give the child time to process what has been said. This gives them time to put their thoughts into words.

Young children with Autism may have difficulty making sense of words and might not be able to make a link between what they see and what is being said. It can help the child if the sentence is divided up into small chunks.

The pupil with Autism may take what is said literally, misunderstand sarcasm and miss out on jokes.

Expressions such as 'You will burst if you eat any more' can frighten the child. It is important to explain sayings like this.

Teach the child that words don't always match emotions – a person might say 'That's great!' in a sarcastic tone, actually meaning 'That's awful.'

TEACHING COMMUNICATION SKILLS

- **Role play greeting a variety of people**, e.g. the head teacher, a friend, a policeman, known adults.

- **Teach about taking turns in a conversation.** In circle time pass round an object or toy. The child can talk when they are holding the toy. Use a timer to show when it is time for someone else to talk.

- **Make an 'interest box'** – put in photos illustrating different subjects, e.g. animals, singers, holiday destinations and sports. Ask the child to choose a card and talk to a partner about the subject.

Some children with Autism use language predominantly to get objects or activities that they want and to get their needs met. The child with Autism needs to be taught how to use language to communicate socially.

Explain that rules change according to the situation, for example, it would be okay to say 'Hi' to a friend but it is not an appropriate form of address to use for the head teacher.

Some children with Autism like to talk about things they are interested in, but they do not realise that other people may not be interested in the subject so they continue talking. Practising skills such as taking turns in a conversation and listening to others when they are talking can be developed through activities in a small group.

SUPPORTING SOCIAL SKILLS

- Children with Autism can have difficulty developing positive peer interactions. Additional adult support is often available in the classroom but support may also be needed in unstructured situations and in the playground.

- Children with Autism can be taught what to do in a given situation but they need to understand why the action or comment is appropriate in order to generalise the skill.

- Social rules can often be confusing and cause anxiety, as many rules are unwritten or not spoken about.

What unwritten social rules can you think of?

Set up a Social Skills Group and include activities to develop skills such as understanding gesture and facial expression. Teach skills of turn taking and sharing toys and equipment. Play games such as the 'Add a sentence' game (start with a sentence and ask each child in the group to add a sentence to create a story). Games like this develop the child's ability to listen to others and respond appropriately.

Children with Autism often find losing particularly difficult to cope with. Explain before a game begins whether there will be a winner or loser. Talk about it being okay to lose and encourage the child to have another go. Show newspaper articles about sports personalities winning or losing a game or race. Children without Autism understand many social rules instinctively, but children with Autism need to be taught them, for example, if the cinema is nearly empty you don't go and sit close to another person. In a lift you don't make eye contact.

Staff Training – Slide 18

SOCIAL INTERACTION

- Babies and young children without Autism seem to know that they can share an activity with others and enjoy this interaction. Some children with Autism may seem more interested in objects rather than people.

- It is important to make social interactions motivating for the pupil.

- Children with Autism may need help to develop positive friendships.

- Many pupils with Autism do not recognise that another person is taking advantage of them, and this can make them vulnerable to bullying and teasing.

The child with Autism may appear to be in a world of their own and not seek out others to share an experience. Others may want to be sociable but don't seem to understand how to do this. Children with Autism often attempt to make social contact and make friends but can get confused or rebuffed. This can lead to the child becoming isolated. It is important to find a balance between encouraging the child to participate in social situations and ensuring they don't become anxious. Many children make friends with someone who has similar interests. Identifying children with similar interests and introducing them to each other or providing break time and lunchtime clubs where children can pursue their interests could be a good way for the pupil with Autism to become involved in a positive social situation.

PLAY

- Through play young children learn a lot of social skills including cooperating with others and working collaboratively.

- Many children become best friends because they have the same interests.

- Children with Autism often have delayed play skills and like to play with children younger than themselves.

For most pupils with Autism, play moves too fast and they struggle to understand the changing rules of a game. Children with Autism often behave as if they are younger than their chronological age and their play skills are delayed, so they like to play with children younger than themselves. Sensory play and rough and tumble games tend to dominate the play of children with Autism. Girls with Autism often join in and follow the play of their peers rather than initiate it.

Children without Autism are able to 'read' a person's character. They work out who will make a good friend. Help the child to understand their own personality and recognise what type of person they may get along with.

Staff Training – Slide 20

A DIFFERENT WAY OF THINKING

Those with ASD may find themselves living in a world dominated by individuals operating from a cognitive mindset quite different to their own. (Lawson 2001, p.15)

Many people believe that children with Autism have a unique thinking style. Some people with Autism have exceptional memories. Young children with Autism can often memorise large chunks of information. It is important to be aware that this can mask their understanding.

Stephen Wiltshire MBE is an artist who draws and paints very detailed cityscapes. He is able to draw a landscape from memory after seeing it just once. After a 20-minute helicopter ride over New York City he was able to remember what he had seen and draw the landscape.

VISUAL PROCESSING

We all learn in different ways. Temple Grandin, who has Autism, says she thinks in pictures:

> words are like a second language to me...when somebody speaks to me, his words are instantly translated into pictures. (Grandin 2006, p.3)

Not everyone with Autism 'thinks in pictures', however many people with Autism are visual learners and using visuals can support their understanding.

ARE YOU A VISUAL THINKER?

Do you use these?

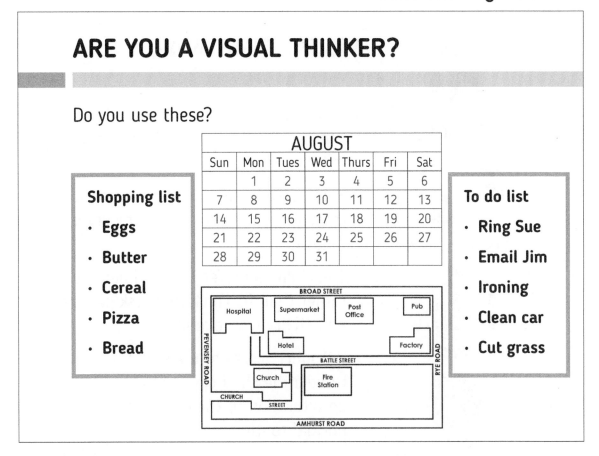

Think how much you use visuals and how reliant you are on them.

Most people understand information more clearly if it is displayed visually but this is especially important for pupils with Autism.

VISUAL TIMETABLE

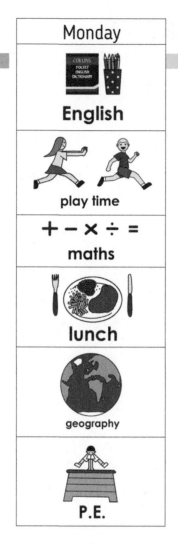

Monday
English
play time
maths
lunch
geography
P.E.

- Using visuals such as a visual timetable will help the child to follow the structure of the day.

- Being able to refer to it throughout the day means the child's anxiety is reduced.

- The child can refer to the timetable rather than be constantly asking when an activity will take place.

- Introduce a **'change card'** to help the child cope with an alteration to their normal routine.

a change

Displaying a visual timetable in the classroom will be very helpful not only for the pupil with Autism, but also for all the other children in the class.

Pupils with Autism like routine and things to be predictable. Therefore, change can make them anxious. Warn pupils about any alterations to the routine of the day or changes in staffing to reduce their anxiety. Using visuals can help to do this, as they are tangible and the pupil can continually refer to them for reassurance. Teaching the pupil that change is okay is important to help to reduce anxiety. Show the child a 'change card' and add it to the visual timetable. The child will still need reassurance, as any transition is difficult for a child with Autism to cope with. The 'change card' is particularly helpful if you are unsure when an event will happen, for example, the arrival time of a visitor.

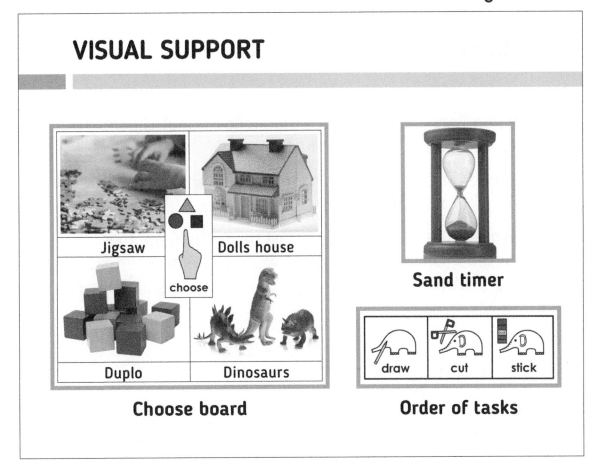

Some other ideas for using visuals to support the child are listed here.

- **Choosing**: A choice board enables the child to initiate the choosing of an activity.

- **Organisation**: An order-of-activities visual can help the child to understand the order in which tasks should be completed.

- **Transition**: Pupils have difficulty with transitions between activities and moving from one area to another and also with larger transitions such as moving class or school. Creating a photo book of the new environment and staff will help reduce anxiety and help them to understand the new situation. Using a sand timer can also help a pupil transition from one activity to another.

THEORY OF MIND

- Baron-Cohen and Bolton (1993) proposed that children with Autism lack a 'Theory of Mind'.

- This is the ability to understand that other people have their own feelings, thoughts, ideas and opinions.

- People without Autism try to see things from another person's perspective. We try to work out what other people are thinking or feeling. This helps us to understand other people.

Baron-Cohen and Bolton (1993) proposed that children with Autism lack a 'Theory of Mind'.

Very young children when they play the game 'peek a boo' often cover their eyes and think that because they can't see you, you can't see them. The child has not yet developed what is called a 'Theory of Mind'. By age 3 most children without Autism are able to understand that other people have their own thoughts, feelings and knowledge. Children with Autism have difficulty with this and may have an underdeveloped or lack of Theory of Mind.

This means that the child with Autism may believe you know what they are thinking or want and not think to explain this to you.

Staff Training – Slide 26

THEORY OF MIND

This can affect the child's ability:

- to understand other people's feelings
- to take into account what other people know
- to understand the reasons behind people's actions or intentions.

People with Autism often lack social awareness and do not pick up on social cues. Baron-Cohen believes the reason for this difficulty and the child's difficulty empathising is that they have not developed a 'Theory of Mind'.

He believes that, 'because children with Autism are unable to think about other people's thoughts, people's actions can appear very confusing to them, since the reasons people do things are often because they think or believe certain things' (Baron-Cohen and Bolton 1993, p.45).

PROCESSING INFORMATION
The ability to regulate, control and manage thoughts and actions

Planning

Organising

Prioritising

Flexible thinking

Self-regulation

'Executive function' refers to the processes that enable us to plan, be organised, focus our attention and have inhibitory control. Executive functioning develops throughout childhood and is only fully developed as the person becomes an adult.

Pupils with Autism have rigid patterns of thinking. They have difficulty accessing information in their memory, considering alternatives and solving problems. If the child is anxious, it can result in them being unable to work out what is happening and make sense of a situation.

Staff Training – Slide 28

PROCESSING INFORMATION

I am so often expected to process more than one thing at any one time. I find this demanding and because it is so difficult to do I can become anxious even thinking of the event. (Lawson 2001, p.98)

Many pupils with Autism find it difficult to interpret and understand information from more than one sense at a time, for example they may have difficulty looking at a person and processing what they are saying at the same time. In the quote, Lawson (2001) describes how processing multiple things at once can be a source of anxiety.

SPECIAL INTERESTS

The pupil will be motivated by their interest and can be highly knowledgeable about it. If possible, incorporate the pupil's interest into the curriculum.

Many pupils with Autism have special interests. Children with Autism can often focus on their special interest for extended periods of time and become very knowledgeable about the subject. If possible, include the pupil's special interest in the curriculum. For many pupils who are very anxious, focusing on their special interest can reduce their high anxiety. However, sometimes the special interest can become all consuming and the child will have difficulty focusing on anything else. This can restrict the child's development and exploration of the environment, and it may be necessary to restrict the time the pupil spends on their special interest.

MOTIVATION

- Praise may not be enough.

- Motivation may not be intrinsic.

- Children with autism may need tangible rewards and motivators.

Reading **Then** Puzzle

'Now/then' visual

'Working for...' visual

Many pupils with Autism are not interested in a social reward, such as a smile from the teacher to show approval or someone saying 'well done'. For many pupils with Autism it will be necessary to find out their special interests and use these to motivate them to complete an activity they are reluctant to do. For some pupils the reward will need to follow the desired behaviour immediately.

A 'now/then' visual can be used as a motivator. Photos or symbols are inserted into a grid with the activity the adult wants the child to complete in the 'now' box and an activity the child likes in the 'then' box. This helps the child to know that when they have completed the adult-directed task they will be rewarded by being able to do a preferred activity.

Others may respond well to a 'working for...' approach where the pupil needs to complete several activities or pieces of work before receiving the agreed reward.

CENTRAL COHERENCE

People with autism may focus on detail and may not see the whole picture or make sense of a situation.

Attwood (2005) suggests that people with Autism lack 'central coherence'. This means that the child with Autism has difficulty connecting concepts and needs help to see the overview or whole picture. The child can often become preoccupied with parts of an object.

Difficulty with central coherence means a pupil may have difficulty working out what is important within a situation, as they will not see the whole, just the parts. It will affect their ability to interpret situations and prioritise.

ABILITY TO FOCUS ON DETAIL

This can be a great strength. There are many jobs that require this skill.

- Air traffic controller

- Proofreader

- Accountant

- Train signalling/train driver/bus driver

- Computer programming

Many individuals with Autism are good at focusing on detail. There are some jobs that require great accuracy and the person to be able to look at fine detail. Many people with Autism are particularly suited to these types of careers.

GENERALISING LEARNING

We tend not to take what we have learnt from one situation and be able to apply it to another. (Lawson 2001, p.38)

This means that every situation is seen as new and this has major implications for the children's ability to generalise their learning.

The thinking of children with Autism is characterised by their difficulty to make meaning of their experiences. Wenn Lawson (writing here as Wendy Lawson) suggests that people with Autism are unable to use their senses in an integrated way and that their processing of information will be different.

To help the child generalise what is being taught, relate it to previous learning, give real-life examples and teach concepts in different situations.

It is important to liaise with parents/carers and other staff to find out what has been learnt at home and in different situations.

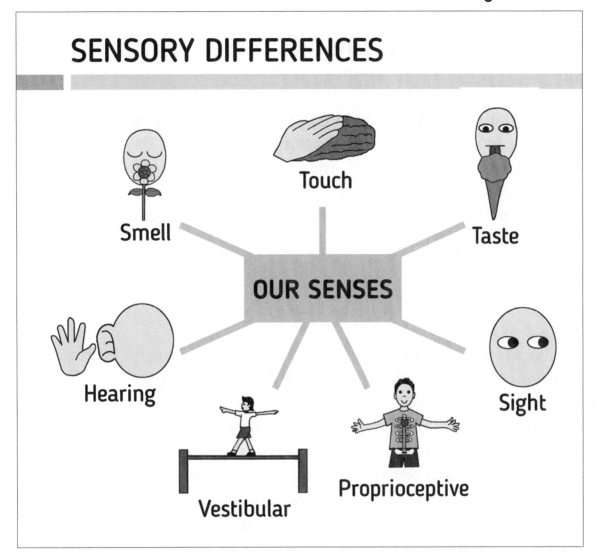

Our senses send messages to our brain that help us interpret our environment. People will recognise the 5 senses of touch, taste, sight, hearing and smell. There are two other senses that are very important for us that help us to interpret and understand our environment.

The vestibular sense gives us information on balance, posture and where our body is in space.

The proprioceptive sense gives us body awareness and information on where our body parts are and how they are moving. It also gives us information on things such as whether we are feeling hot, cold or hungry.

SUPPORTING SENSORY DIFFERENCES

What I do realise is that I do not see the world as others do. Most people take the routines of the life and day to day connections for granted, The fact that they can see, hear, smell, touch and relate to others is 'normal'. For me these things are often painfully overwhelming, non existent or just confusing. (Lawson 2001, p.2)

This is a quote by Wenn Lawson, who has Autism, describing the effect sensory difficulties have on his ability to cope day to day. If there are problems processing and integrating information from their senses the child may display unusual reactions to stimuli. Sometimes what we consider a harmless sensory stimulus could cause the child with Autism's brain to trigger the 'freeze, fight/flight' response. They may be unable to modulate their responses and may underreact or overreact to the situation. This may result in the child withdrawing, trying to escape by running away, or having an extreme response to the situation. The child may be frightened and may react by screaming or hitting themselves or others.

Staff Training – Slide 36

SENSORY INTEGRATION

- We take in millions of bits of sensory information each day.

- The ability to take all this in, know what is important, store what we need for future use and discard the rest is called **sensory integration**. It is the ability of our senses to work together.

The brain is constantly receiving and processing information from the senses. We have billions of nerve cells called neurons. Networks of cells are created as we learn things. Messages from the senses are processed in specialised parts of the brain.

Babies have to learn to make meaning of sensory information through exploring their environment. Children with Autism often have difficulty processing input from the sensory systems. These difficulties can affect any of the senses.

It is through interactions with our environment that we develop the ability to know, for example, the scent of an onion without seeing it or to know a brick is heavy without picking it up.

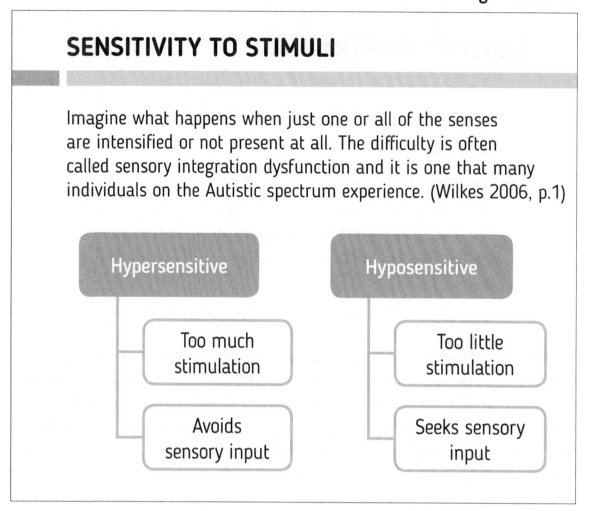

SENSITIVITY TO STIMULI

Imagine what happens when just one or all of the senses are intensified or not present at all. The difficulty is often called sensory integration dysfunction and it is one that many individuals on the Autistic spectrum experience. (Wilkes 2006, p.1)

Hypersensitive
- Too much stimulation
- Avoids sensory input

Hyposensitive
- Too little stimulation
- Seeks sensory input

Some pupils may be oversensitive (hypersensitive) or undersensitive (hyposensitive), and this can affect any of the senses. When the child has too much sensory information to process, they may be unable to interpret their surroundings and make sense of a situation.

They often need extra time to process sensory information.

THE SENSES OF TOUCH AND SIGHT

TOUCH

SIGHT

Touch: Hypersensitivity could mean the child dislikes things on their hands and feet, dislikes certain textures of clothes and finds touch painful.

Hyposensitivity can be a cause of self-harming and sensory-seeking behaviours, with the child constantly touching objects and people.

Sight: Hypersensitivity could mean the child is sensitive to sunlight or electric lighting.

Hyposensitivity could mean the child intently studies objects or people. The child may seek to create movement in front of their eyes, for example, by watching a handful of sand slip through their fingers or taking a toy car close to their eyes and spinning the wheels.

THE SENSE OF HEARING

HEARING

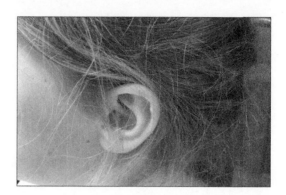

When two people are talking at once, it is difficult for me to screen out one voice and listen to the other. My ears are like microphones picking up all sounds with equal intensity. Most people's ears are like highly directional microphones, which only pick up sounds from the person they are pointed at. In a noisy place I can't understand speech, because I cannot screen out background noise. (Grandin 1996, p.68)

Hearing: Hypersensitivity can mean the child may hear sounds we can't hear, being very sensitive to noises and screaming in response to certain sounds.

Temple Grandin, who has Autism, describes how, as a child, loud noises felt to her like a dentist's drill hitting a nerve and actually caused her pain.

We are able to filter sounds and decide what is important. We don't pay attention to every sound, but we know when to take notice of a sound, for example, someone yelling for help. Many children with Autism cannot do this and can easily become overwhelmed. In the quote Temple Grandin explains her inability to cut out particular sounds. This can have a big impact in the classroom, as the child may not be able to filter out sounds in order to listen to the teacher.

THE SENSES OF SMELL AND TASTE

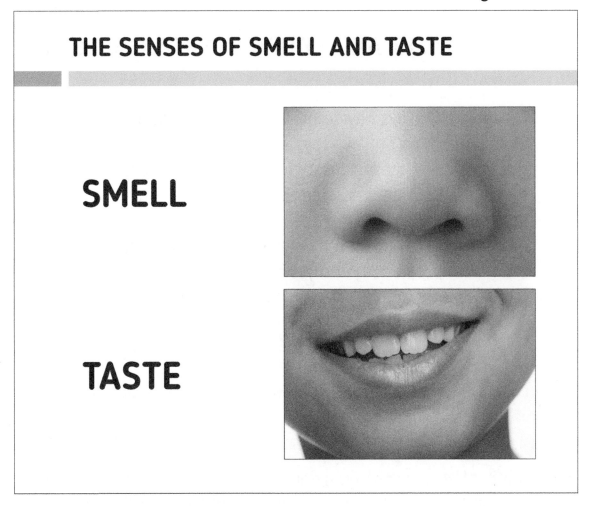

SMELL

TASTE

Smell: Hypersensitivity to smells means they can be overpowering. The child may, for example, dislike perfumes, soaps or cooking smells.

Hyposensitivity can mean the child doesn't respond to smells. They could seek extra sensory input by smelling everything around them.

Taste: Many children with Autism have restricted diets, which can be due to hypersensitivity to certain textures of food.

Hyposensitivity could mean the child eats objects that are not edible.

VESTIBULAR AND PROPRIOCEPTIVE SENSES

I seemed to always have a need to move, climb tall trees, and spin around on lawn toys and otherwise seek activities that provided a lot of sensory input. Today an occupational therapist would diagnose me as being hyposensitive in the vestibular and proprioceptive senses. In other words I needed more stimulation by movement and deep pressure than most people to find myself within the environment. (Shore 2006, p.202)

Vestibular: Children who are hypersensitive may find it difficult to balance on apparatus and become frightened.

To get extra sensory input the child may rock or spin round and round.

Proprioceptive: Hypersensitivity can result in the child being uncoordinated.

Hyposensitivity can result in a lack of body sensations and the child will be unaware when, for example, they are too hot or cold. Many children with Autism have a reduced perception of pain and may lack awareness of their own safety.

Staff Training – Slide 42

NEUROLOGICAL DIFFERENCES

Bogdashina believes that:

> the sensory problems in autism are often overlooked. As children are unable to cope with the demands of the world they are not equipped to deal with, they are likely to display behavioural problems, such as self stimulation, self injury, aggression, avoidance, rigidity, high anxiety, panic attacks, etc. It is important to remember these children have no control over their problems as they are caused by neurological differences. (Bogdashina 2003, p.170)

Some children become fascinated by a sensory stimulus and will continually seek that sensation. Although this is very calming for them, it can restrict exploration and development of play.

Some children may have different reactions to a stimulus depending on what demands are being placed on them: they could scream one day when they hear a certain sound and not react another.

Sensory difficulties can easily lead to overload and the child reacting by withdrawing, isolating themselves or displaying challenging behaviour.

SUPPORTING BEHAVIOUR

...every waking moment is devoted to trying to sort out what is going on and to formulate a response to it... (Montgomery 1997, p.23)

- For pupils with ASD stress can be the major underlying factor contributing to difficulties in communication, socialization and academic performance.

- Stress can impact every aspect of your life.

It is our job to decrease the stress as much as possible through structure and predictability.

Pupils with Autism often have high levels of stress. Children with Autism often try to control people and their environment, as this helps them to make a situation more predictable.

Discuss:

- What you do when you are feeling stressed?

- Do you struggle to concentrate or think of solutions to a problem?

- Do you become less social than usual, for example, trying to avoid talking to someone you may see in the supermarket?

- Do you retreat to your happy place, for example, your bedroom, bathroom, garden shed?

Staff Training – Slide 44

IMPACT OF STRESS

- For pupils with ASD stress can be the major underlying factor contributing to difficulties in communication, socialization and academic performance.

When stress levels get too high the child may display a range of behaviours such as:

- withdrawing

- displaying repetitive behaviours such as hand flapping, rocking or repeating vocal sounds such as humming or repeating the same word or phrase

- shouting

- running away.

IDEAS FOR COPING STRATEGIES

- Go to my safe place.
- Squeeze stress ball or play dough.
- Take deep breaths and count to 10.
- Look at photos of favourite images.
- Think about favourite people, places or activities.
- Do some drawing.
- Do some physical exercise.
- Play with a ball.
- Have a drink through a straw.

Schools are often noisy, busy environments and the child with Autism may need to be taught coping strategies. Help the child to identify things that make them calm and make a list of them as a visual prompt. Encourage the child to go to lunch clubs, the library or areas in the environment that are quiet. Teach the child how to use an 'exit' card to go to a safe place. Rehearse going there when the pupil is calm. Identify which staff the pupil can talk to when they are anxious.

SUPPORTIVE BEHAVIOUR

Remain calm

- Do not raise your voice – use a lower but firm tone of voice.

Be aware of possible triggers

- Avoid these settings and triggers if at all possible.

- Reduce your expectations of behaviour if the child is anxious.

- If a child displays challenging behaviour, then analyse the situation as they may require visual support to cope in the social situation.

Become a detective. All behaviour is a form of communication. It is important to think about what the pupil is trying to communicate and what may be causing the behaviour. To try and work out what is causing or triggering a behaviour, it can be helpful to use an ABC chart.

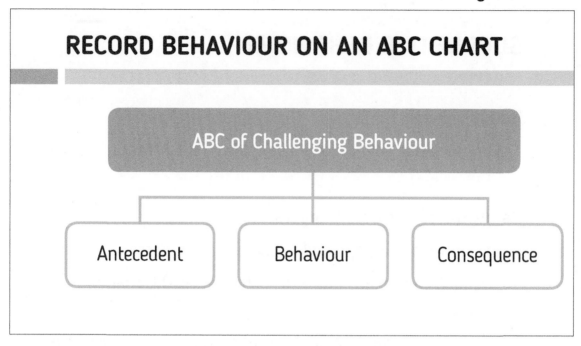

Record on the ABC chart:

A = Antecedent: Describe what happened before the behaviour, who was involved and where the behaviour took place.

B = Behaviour: Describe what the child did.

C = Consequences: Describe what happened after the behaviour and how the child and others reacted.

Analysing the ABC chart can often help identify the reason for a particular behaviour.

When the reason that a pupil is exhibiting a challenging behaviour has been established, an alternative and more acceptable way for achieving that purpose can be developed.

TEACH CHILDREN TO RECOGNISE THEIR EMOTIONS

happy

sad

- Children with autism often have difficulty recognising their feelings.

- It is important to help the child recognise when they are angry and recognise the situations that make them angry.

angry

worried

- Explain that it is ok to feel angry but not ok to react in such a way that others get hurt, property gets damaged or they hurt themselves.

Teaching pupils to identify their own and others' emotions is very important. It is important to label the child's emotion if you know what it is, as they may not be able to recognise it themselves. For example:

'I can see you are angry because your model has broken.'

'I can see you are worried about going into assembly.'

You can also describe how you are feeling. For example:

'I feel sad when you take all the cars and don't share them.'

'I am feeling happy because you have finished your work.'

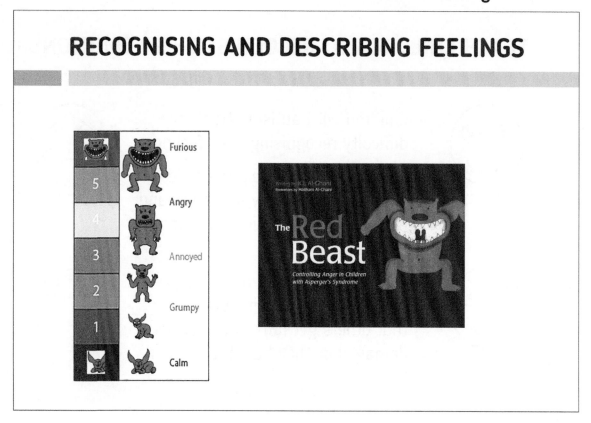

Using a visual scale can help the child to recognise and describe how they are feeling. This example is taken from the book *The Red Beast* by Kay Al-Ghani. Many pupils will need to work with an adult to help them identify how they are feeling. The pupil can record how they are feeling at each point on the scale and the situations that might cause these feelings. They can also describe how their body reacts in these situations.

Through identification of these emotions, the pupil can begin to self-regulate their emotions and their behaviour.

Staff Training – Slide 50

PROMOTING POSITIVE BEHAVIOUR

- Praise the child for positive behaviour.
- If a pupil is displaying inappropriate behaviour distract and redirect.
- Support transitions.
- Be consistent.

Often, when children are behaving well we ignore them and it is only when they misbehave that they get attention. It is important to praise positive behaviour and say why you like the behaviour.

Showing an object that the child likes or talking about the child's interest may distract them from displaying an inappropriate behaviour and enable the child to calm down and move on to another activity.

Transitions can cause anxiety. Give a warning of any change. Many children need to carry a transitional object with them to change from one activity to another or from one environment to another.

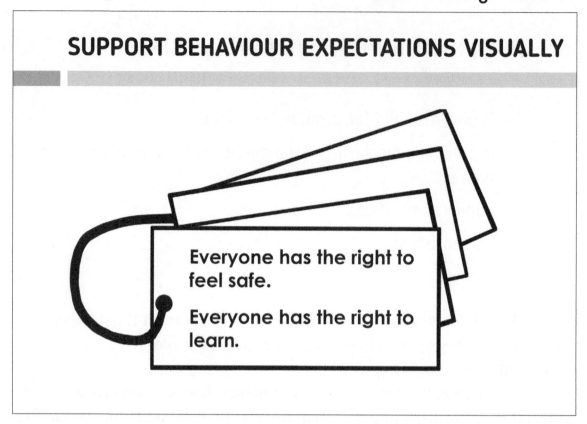

Visually presenting school rules can help the pupil understand and remember them.

Staff Training – Slide 52

WHAT EVERY CHILD WITH AUTISM WISHES YOU KNEW

Work to view my autism as a different ability rather than a disability. Look past what you may see as limitations and see the gifts autism has given me. (Notbohm 2007, p.xxxi)

Ellen Notbohm is a parent of a child with Autism. This quote comes from her book, *Ten Things Every Child with Autism Wishes You Knew*.

Think about ways you can use and develop the positive qualities of pupils with Autism in your school.

ACTIVITY: THINK ABOUT THE CHILD

Reflect on what you have learnt and complete the activity sheet.

- List the child's strengths and interests.

- Consider how you can support the child.

SOCIAL COMMUNICATION

The pupil may take things literally and have difficulty understanding jokes and sarcasm. They may struggle to understand verbal and non-verbal communication, for example, gesture, facial expression, body language, and tone of voice.

I can help by:

SOCIAL RELATIONSHIPS

The pupil may find some social situations difficult to cope with and this could result in a particular behaviour to try to avoid a situation. Difficulty understanding social rules can lead to problems making and sustaining friendships.

I can help by:

STRENGTHS AND INTERESTS

SOCIAL IMAGINATION

The world often appears very unpredictable and the pupil finds comfort in routines they can control. They may become distressed over small changes in routines or the environment. The pupil may have difficulty predicting future events.

I can help by:

SENSORY

Many children may be hypersensitive to certain sensations or have low sensitivity. The pupil may need extra time to process sensory information and may not be able to filter sounds or prioritise what is important.

I can help by:

This activity could be done individually or in groups. Give out 'Resource 16: Staff resource: Thinking about the child' and ask staff to think about the child's strengths and interests and then consider what support the child may need.

PART 3

DEVELOPING A SUPPORTIVE TEAM

INVOLVING THE CHILD WITH AUTISM

INVOLVING THE CHILD IN DEVELOPING THE PEER AWARENESS ASSEMBLY AND LESSONS

Children without Autism often notice that the child with Autism reacts differently to situations and struggle to understand why. Knowing about the child's diagnosis will help them to make sense of why the child is behaving in that way and also why the staff may treat them differently.

Stobart (2009) believes that: 'Understanding promotes tolerance. Inclusion is not about pretending that everyone is the same; it's about understanding, accommodating people's differences' (Stobart 2009, p.12).

When children without Autism know about the differences Autism creates they can support their classmate in situations they find difficult. Children with Autism can be vulnerable to bullying, but changing peers' attitudes to difference should make them less of a target and give them a support group who will look out for them.

DISCUSSIONS WITH PUPILS WITH AUTISM

Discussions should take place with both the child with Autism and their family. It is vital to respect the pupil's views and no Autism peer awareness programme should identify the child if they do not wish to disclose that they have a diagnosis. Some pupils may have been told at a very young age that they have Autism and others may have received a recent diagnosis; children respond differently to finding this out. It is important for staff to help the child accept and recognise the positives of their diagnosis. Talk to the pupil about whether they want their peers to know they have Autism or would prefer the Autism peer awareness programme to be covered without any reference to them, with the lessons forming part of a scheme of work focusing on celebrating and accepting difference. Discuss whether the pupil wishes to be involved in the delivery of the assembly or lessons or if they would rather withdraw from the session. Discuss what, if any, information they would like to share with their peers.

PROMPT LIST FOR THE CHILD WITH AUTISM TO CONSIDER

Some of the things you might like to share with your peers are:

- your special interests and what you like to do

- your strengths

- things you find difficult to understand

- times and situations that you find difficult to cope with

- things you would like others to help you with.

Two examples of what pupils have said about themselves and how others could help them are given below. A blank handout is provided for pupils to complete in 'Resource 15: Pupil resource: Things about me I would like to share with my classmates'.

THINGS ABOUT ME I WOULD LIKE TO SHARE WITH MY CLASSMATES

ABOUT ME	Strengths and interests	Things I find difficult
	I like playing chasing and football in the playground.	Sometimes I get angry when we have to stop our game and come back into class.
	I am very good at remembering facts and I know a lot about space travel.	I don't understand why people are not interested when I tell them all the facts I know.
	Maths and Science are my favourite subjects.	I get upset when people change the timetable.
	I have got lots of joke books and I like reading them.	I often don't know when other people are joking.

THINGS I WOULD LIKE MY CLASSMATES TO HELP ME WITH

* Please warn me when it is nearly the end of playtime.

* Before telling me a joke say 'I'm joking.'

* When you can see I am getting anxious remind me to use my 'Take a break' card.

* Give me time to answer your questions.

THINGS ABOUT ME I WOULD LIKE TO SHARE WITH MY CLASSMATES

ABOUT ME	Strengths and interests	Things I find difficult
	I am very good at reading and spelling.	Sometimes I get confused if it is noisy in the classroom and can't understand what to do.
	I like talking to my friend at playtime.	I don't like playing games with lots of people and sometimes I get anxious and need to be on my own.
	I love dancing and PE.	I find it difficult to sit still in class.
	I love drawing and like to do detailed drawings.	I like to do things perfectly and can get upset if I am not happy with my work.

THINGS I WOULD LIKE MY CLASSMATES TO HELP ME WITH

* Try not to be noisy in the classroom.

* If you see that I am confused, explain to me what I have to do.

* When I am anxious, showing me visually helps.

* When I get upset about my work, give me time to calm down.

* Don't get offended if I don't want to play with you because I need to be on my own. I still want to be your friend.

PARTNERSHIP WITH PARENTS/CARERS

Working in partnership with parents is vital to ensure the best outcomes for the child. Parents and carers know their child best and are a valuable source of expertise and information. Regular meetings for information sharing will ensure successful strategies are shared and any difficulties identified and addressed early.

The book *Dignity and Inclusion* describes the responsibility that professionals have regarding information sharing: 'Personal information about children and families held by professionals is subject to a duty of confidence and should normally not be disclosed without consent' (Carlin, Delamore and Allard 2014, p.72).

Parents have differing views on telling their child about a diagnosis of Autism, and their views must be respected. Some parents like to explain the diagnosis to their child in a simplistic way when they are very young and others prefer to wait until they believe their child will be able to understand it better. This means that some pupils in primary schools who have a diagnosis of Autism will not have been told, which means any Autism awareness training will need to be delivered sensitively as part of a module on 'understanding difference' in a personal, emotional and social teaching module. In this circumstance, care must be taken that the pupil can not be identified.

Parents often say that they have encountered negative attitudes and lack of understanding about their child's behaviour in the community and obviously they worry that other people knowing about their child's diagnosis may lead to them being isolated. However, we have found that providing information on Autism for adults and children who meet their child leads to greater understanding and acceptance.

Arranging a meeting with the family to find out their views and to establish how much knowledge about Autism the child has is essential. Discussing any potential factors that contribute to a pupil's anxiety and jointly agreeing what would help the child develop positive social interactions will bring about better outcomes for the child. Working together on a plan to implement the programme, agreeing what information is to be shared and asking what support they think would benefit their child will enable the school community's awareness and understanding that leads to changes in attitude to develop. It is vitally important that the views of the child have been sought and are respected in the delivering of the peer awareness assembly and lessons. The child could be involved in all or part of the parent/carer discussion meeting or their views could be sought earlier.

SUGGESTED FORMAT: LETTER TO PARENTS/CARERS

This letter can be adapted to be sent to either an individual parent or a group of parents inviting them to participate in a meeting to see the assembly and lesson plan materials and contribute their ideas on the best way to support their children.

Dear _____,

At _____ School we are working on changing attitudes to Autism. We believe it is vital to increase awareness and sensitivity towards children with Autism and look at how children can support their peers and accept difference.

We are going to be delivering a whole-school assembly to raise awareness of Autism, which will form part of our personal and social curriculum module focusing on difference. Following the assembly, lessons will be delivered raising awareness of Autism and ways the other children in the class could support their peers. Children will be asked for their ideas on how to ensure that school is a fun and positive place for a child on the spectrum to be.

Through this initiative we believe pupils will be more empathetic, as they will have gained a greater understanding of the strengths and differences of the pupil with Autism. We hope that this will lead to pupils with Autism having a support network and more positive interactions with their peers.

We would like to invite you to a meeting to discuss this and to find out whether your child would prefer others not to know that they have Autism and if they would like to have input into the assembly and lessons.

Please phone me on _____ to arrange a convenient date for the meeting.

If you are unable to attend a meeting, please could you complete the attached questionnaire [attach 'Resource 14: Parent resource: Questionnaire for the family'] and return it to me.

Thank you.
Yours sincerely,

_____

SUGGESTED FORMAT: RECORD OF PARENT/CARER MEETING

Name of child _____

Class _____ Date of meeting _____

People attending meeting:

Date pupil received diagnosis _____

Does pupil know about their diagnosis?   **yes/ no**

Following an explanation of the Peer Awareness Assembly/Programme, if the child is aware of their diagnosis, ask these questions:

- Are you happy for your child to be asked if they wish to be involved in the Assembly/Programme?   **yes/no**

- What strengths and interests does your child have?

- What issues does your child have at school?

- How do you think your child could be supported by his/her peers?

- What information are you happy to be shared with your child's peers?

Pupil's views:

Parents'/carers' views:

CREATING CHAMPIONS FOR AUTISM

CASE STUDY

This case study describes the impact of a whole-school assembly and peer awareness lessons in a primary school. The school had been particularly concerned about two pupils who were having great difficulty at playtime and with social skills in general. The assembly and lessons were delivered by an outreach worker from an Inclusion Support Service that supports children with Autism in mainstream schools. The peer awareness lessons were delivered to children who had volunteered to join the sessions to find out ways to support their classmates.

Transcript of an interview with the outreach worker who implemented the peer awareness programme

Did you have any comments from children following the whole-school Autism assembly?

One of the children approached me after the assembly to say that he had Asperger Syndrome but had not told anyone. He later disclosed to his class that he had Asperger Syndrome and when I saw him again he said it had made a lot of difference to the way the other children spoke to him.

Another little girl came to tell me that she had a younger brother in a special school with Autism and she was very keen to be included in the Autism Champions group.

Did you notice any changes in attitude of the volunteers when you were delivering the peer awareness lessons?

The Year 6 students participated well in the weekly sessions and said they looked forward to them. At the end of the course they expressed regret that it was over and they were very proud to have earned their badges.

What ideas did the volunteers suggest of ways they could support their peers with Autism in class?

The pupil volunteers suggested:

- Ask if they understood what work they had to do.

- Use pictures to help them understand better.

- Request a break for them if I see they are becoming anxious.

- Encourage everyone not to be too noisy.

- Be kind and be their friend.

What ideas did the volunteers suggest of ways to support their peers with Autism at playtimes or during lunchtime?

The volunteers suggested:

- Friendship benches in the playground.

- Special lunch clubs about the child with Autism's special interests but open to other children too.

- Trying to look out for the child with Autism so they wouldn't get bullied.

- Suggest the child sits down and has water if they look overexcited.

- Take the child into class before playtime ends so they don't have to queue.

- Have a lunch table in a quiet area where I could sit with them.

- Have a special running track painted all around the playground for them to focus on if they want to run fast.

- Have a wall that the child could draw on with chalk.

- Provide ear defenders.

- Have some games equipment especially for them.

Did you notice any changes in the behaviour of the children with Autism you were supporting through your outreach work at the school following the peer awareness intervention?

The children I were supporting found playtimes and school more enjoyable and incidents regarding unacceptable behaviour were greatly reduced.

Did you receive any comments from staff?

Staff reported that children with ASD settled better and were less likely to get upset at playtimes and lunchtimes. They noticed greater maturity of attitude towards work and fellow pupils by the Autism Champions.

What are your views on the value of delivering the peer awareness assembly and lessons?

I have found that the peer awareness assemblies have had a positive effect on children and staff. Children with ASD who were reticent about disclosure all felt the assembly had given them self-esteem and confidence. The children who attended the lessons gained confidence and understanding and were eager to pass on the information they learned. It is hoped that these children would take this knowledge into their secondary schools and into the community.

VIEWS OF CHILDREN, STAFF AND PARENTS WHO HAVE BEEN INVOLVED WITH THE STAFF TRAINING AND PEER AWARENESS INTERVENTION IN OTHER SCHOOLS

Impact of the peer awareness programme

Children, staff and parents were asked their opinion on the peer awareness assembly and lessons.

'I feel people understand me better.' Pupil

'My son is happier going to school and says he has friends at playtime now.' Parent

IMPACT ON PUPILS WITH AUTISM

'Huge difference – the impact has been a better experience of learning and a better experience of being part of their school community.' Head teacher

'I was worried about telling people I had Asperger's but it has been good.' Pupil

'Through explaining to the class about Autism they have worked out ways to help their friend with Autism.' Teacher

IMPACT ON PEERS

'Pupils are more actively engaged in supporting each other.' Teacher

'I think they are more understanding and they now realise that T's angry reaction is not directed at them but that he is getting anxious as he didn't understand the rules of the game.' Teacher

'Developing understanding and changing attitudes has been a challenge but also one of our biggest successes.' SENCO

IMPACT ON STAFF

'Through using the Autism awareness materials with my class it has been like opening a door to [name]'s world.' Teacher

'I think it has helped everyone in the school to recognise the gifts and talents of all children and value them.' Teacher

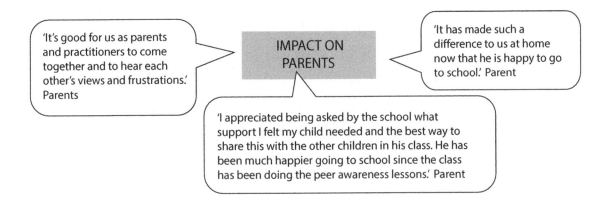

Creating an inclusive school

The term 'integration' was first used in the Warnock Report (Warnock 1978) and this referred to a concept of children with special educational needs being fitted into the education system that existed in the school. Over the years this concept began to alter to the idea of education changing so that it encompassed all children and the term 'inclusion' began to be used more frequently:

> Inclusive education is a process involving restructuring of the curriculum and classroom organisation. This distinguishes it from integration which focuses on the placement of an individual or group having to adapt to what the school is able to offer. (Barnard, Prior and Potter 2000, p.6)

Vision

Charman *et al.* (2011, p.42) identified the following as good practice in Autism education:

> Strong leadership and vision, which saw their school as fully inclusive and deeply embedded within the local community, taking on an ambassadorial role to raise awareness about Autism.

Commitment

Members of schools' leadership teams emphasised their commitment to inclusion and stressed that they felt they were a key factor in influencing others' attitudes. Some emphasised that it needed senior management team, governors, teaching staff, support staff – in fact everyone involved with the child – to have the same commitment. This is confirmed in the government's strategy *Removing Barriers to Achievement* (2004), which describes effective inclusion as relying on more than specialist skills and resources and also needing a positive attitude and greater responsiveness to individual needs and, most importantly, a willingness for all staff to play their part.

All the school leaders interviewed felt it was important to acknowledge diversity, whereas some stressed that you had to go one step further and *celebrate* diversity. Stobart (2009, p.12) concurs with this, stating, 'A school with a culture that celebrates difference will be more successfully inclusive.' One head teacher emphasised that if we wanted to bring about an understanding of difference and tolerance of others in our society, it was important that this was first established in school.

Confidence

Building the confidence of staff was considered an important element in the development of an inclusive school. One head described the attitude of his staff as follows.

'It is very satisfying to see staff with the skills and confidence to support the needs of all the children in their classes.'

CONFIDENCE

'We share a "can do" attitude to removing barriers to learning for children with Autism.'

Partnership

Leadership teams emphasised the benefits of partnership working with parents. Leaders recognised their role in developing partnerships that incorporated the sharing of good practice. It was stressed that the skill was in developing the confidence of all involved with the child.

'It's about having people on board – our best work is when we work as a team.' SENCO

PARTNERSHIP WORKING

'We build up trust and that gives good working relationships.' Assistant Head

A factor identified as helpful was the time to talk, reflect and brainstorm solutions. A SENCO mentioned that 'just being there' and facilitating discussions that allowed for the bouncing of ideas around and sharing strategies was a valuable part of the partnership.

Flexibility

All leaders interviewed stressed the importance of flexibility and the ability to change and adapt their provision to suit individual needs. They promoted the use of an eclectic approach, choosing the best from a range of diverse strategies dependent on the situation rather than relying on a particular intervention.

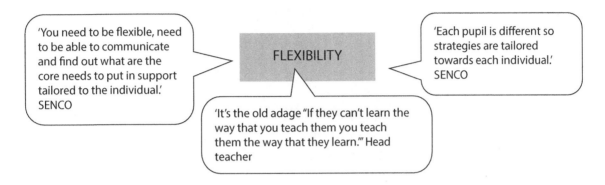

'You need to be flexible, need to be able to communicate and find out what are the core needs to put in support tailored to the individual.' SENCO

FLEXIBILITY

'Each pupil is different so strategies are tailored towards each individual.' SENCO

'It's the old adage "If they can't learn the way that you teach them you teach them the way that they learn."' Head teacher

Following the development of the peer awareness training for staff resources, my overriding thought is that the people I worked with had a passion to make a difference and succeed with the children they were working with, and this enthusiasm inspired others.

CREATING CHAMPIONS: CHANGING ATTITUDES TO AUTISM

Consider whether the the following statements are true to evaluate how inclusive your school is for children with Autism.

- All staff have a raised awareness of Autism.

- All staff promote a positive attitude to difference.

- All staff have a commitment to including children with Autism in the life of the school.

- All staff have a commitment to partnership working with parents.

- All staff understand the importance of flexibility and are willing to change and adapt their provision to suit individual needs.

- The child with Autism has been involved in identifying strategies that would help them.

- Peers have a raised awareness of Autism.

- Peers are involved in assisting children with Autism to participate successfully in the life of the school.

Ask staff to discuss and think about how inclusive their school is and then complete 'Resource 17: Staff resource: How inclusive is your school? questionnaire'.

PART 4

FURTHER RESOURCES

PHOTOCOPIABLE/ DOWNLOADABLE RESOURCES

These resources can be photocopied or downloaded from www.jkp.com/voucher using the code BEANEYAUTISM.

1. A-U-T-I-S-M assembly cards
2. Lesson 1 quiz: How do you like to learn?
3. Lesson 1: How do you learn best?
4. Lesson 2: Cards for non-verbal actions
5. Lesson 2: 'Oh' resource
6. Lesson 2: Idiom cards
7. Lesson 3: Sensory stimulation listening activity
8. Lesson 3: Taste bud experiment
9. Lesson 3: Glasses for sensory stimulation – using peripheral vision
10. Lesson 3: How might sensory differences affect your classmate?
11. Lesson 4: Feelings circle
12. Lesson 4: Worry symbol and cards
13. Lesson 6: Autism Champion
14. Parent resource: Questionnaire for the family
15. Pupil resource: Things about me I would like to share with my classmates
16. Staff resource: Thinking about the child
17. Staff resource: How inclusive is your school? questionnaire

Accept

Understand

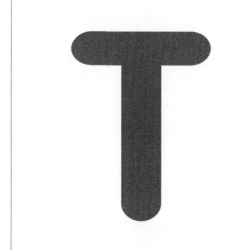

Try to help

I

I
Include me in what you do

S

S
Show support

M

M
Make friends

2. LESSON 1 QUIZ: HOW DO YOU LIKE TO LEARN?

People like to learn in different ways. Some people have strengths in one way of learning.

Tick the boxes that describe you best.

visual learner	☐ I remember information better when I write things down or draw it. ☐ I learn things better by reading information. ☐ When I want to explain something I draw it or write it down. ☐ I read the instructions or look at the diagrams when I get something new. ☐ When I am learning a spelling I like to write it down. ☐ I can visualise a picture in my head.
auditory learner	☐ I remember information better when I listen to it. ☐ When I want to explain something I talk to someone. ☐ I ask people when I want information or I am trying to find out how things work. ☐ I can think better if I talk through my ideas. ☐ To learn a spelling I sound it out in my head.
kinaesthetic learner	☐ I remember information better when I can make or build things. ☐ I can think better when I move about. ☐ I like working with my hands. ☐ When I try to remember something I like to move around. ☐ I like to make models about the topics I am learning about. ☐ I learn better by doing things myself.

Learning Styles	What sort of learner are you? _____

3. LESSON 1: HOW DO YOU LEARN BEST?

What sort of learner are you?

I learn best when	I can look at a visual timetable	I work in a quiet place
I can use a plan or a visual map	I work in a clutter-free space	I have a checklist
I have a reward chart	I have time to think	I know how much time I have to complete a task
I am able to take a movement break	I work on my own	I work in a group
I work with a partner	I work with an adult	I can do my work on the computer

Choose 5 things that will help you be ready to learn and stick the pictures in the boxes.

Name: Draw a picture of yourself in this box.	

4. LESSON 2: CARDS FOR NON-VERBAL ACTIONS

Activity: Either ask the whole group to do the activity or ask a volunteer to choose a card with an instruction written on it and demonstrate the body language to illustrate it. The rest of class can guess what the non-verbal body language is showing.

Show me you are worried e.g. biting lip
Show me you are bored e.g. look up and yawn
Do not touch anyone but using just your hands show me you are angry e.g. clenched fist
Show me you are confident and in control e.g. stand up very straight, hands on hips
Show me you are paying attention e.g. sit up straight and look the person in the eye
Without using words ask me to be quiet e.g. finger on lips, hunch shoulders
Without using words attract my attention to something e.g. beckon, point, wave arms
Show me you are joking e.g. wink

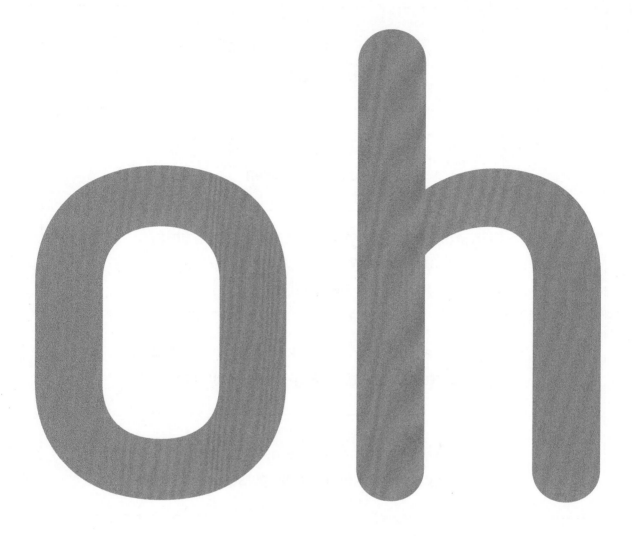

6. LESSON 2: IDIOM CARDS

Cut along the dotted lines and fold in half.

Give each child a saying and ask them to illustrate it. When the children have drawn their images get them to ask the others if they know the meaning of their saying.

You have a chip on your shoulder	**You are upset over something that happened some time ago**
Stop beating around the bush	**Stop avoiding the issue**
You have hit the nail on the head	**You have said or done the correct thing**
It's a piece of cake	**It is easy**
Bend over backwards	**Willing to do anything to help**
Hold your horses	**Wait, be patient**
Keep an eye on him	**Carefully watch him**
To let the cat out the bag	**To tell a secret that you were not supposed to**

7. LESSON 3: SENSORY SIMULATION LISTENING ACTIVITY

This activity is to illustrate what it is like when you can't filter out certain sounds.

Instructions

- Number the pupils 1 or 2.
- Give out a blue, green, black and red crayon to each pupil.
- Tell the pupils that if they are numbered 1 to follow the instructions given by reader 1 and those numbered 2 should listen to reader 2.
- Readers should try to read at the same pace.
- Whilst reading the instructions below, play loud music.

Reader 1 instructions

- Listen carefully to the instructions.
- Draw a black face in the middle of your page.
- Around the face draw a red square.
- Draw a green triangle above the red square.
- Draw a blue rectangle to the right of the red square.
- Draw a green circle to the left of the square.

Reader 2 instructions

- Listen carefully to the instructions.
- Draw a red square in the middle of your page.
- Draw a green triangle above the red square.
- Draw a blue rectangle to the right of the red square.
- Draw a green circle to the left of the red square.
- Draw a black face in the middle of the red square.

Explain to pupils that many people with autism find it difficult to filter sounds. This makes it difficult to follow instructions given by the teacher in the classroom when there are other noises in the background.

8. LESSON 3: TASTE BUD EXPERIMENT

Look at your tongue in a mirror. You have taste buds that identify whether the food is bitter, salty, sweet or sour. Different parts of the tongue identify these.

Experiment with trying different foods to see if they are bitter, salty, sweet or sour. Draw the food item. Put a tick if you like the food and a cross if you don't like it.

Taste buds on the tongue

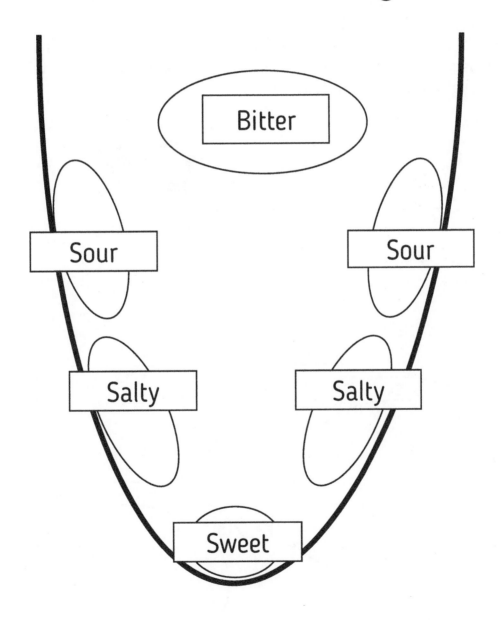

9. LESSON 3: GLASSES FOR SENSORY SIMULATION – USING PERIPHERAL VISION

Instructions for making the glasses

- Cut out glasses and the 2 black circles.

- Cut out lens area.

- Lay glasses in between laminating pouch.

- Place circles in the centre of the lens and laminate.

- Cut out laminated glasses.

Instructions for using the glasses

Ask the child to put on the glasses and try to read a sentence in a book. With the centre of the glasses' lens covered the child cannot see directly ahead of them but will have to use peripheral vision to read the text.

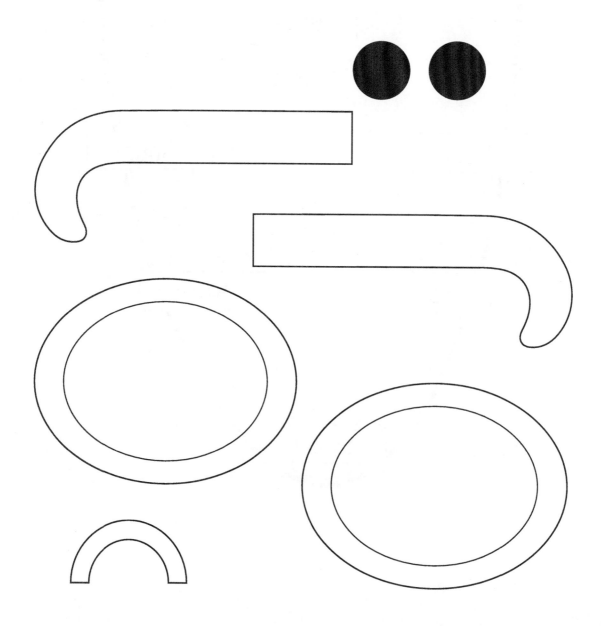

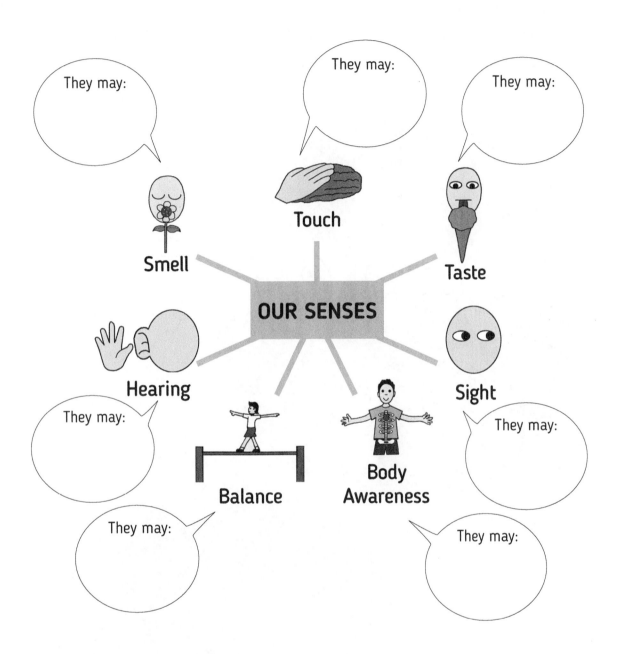

11. LESSON 4: FEELINGS CIRCLE

Instructions

- Cut out the two circles.
- Cover the circle showing the pictures of our feelings with the circle saying 'I feel'.
- Insert a split pin into the centre to join the two circles.

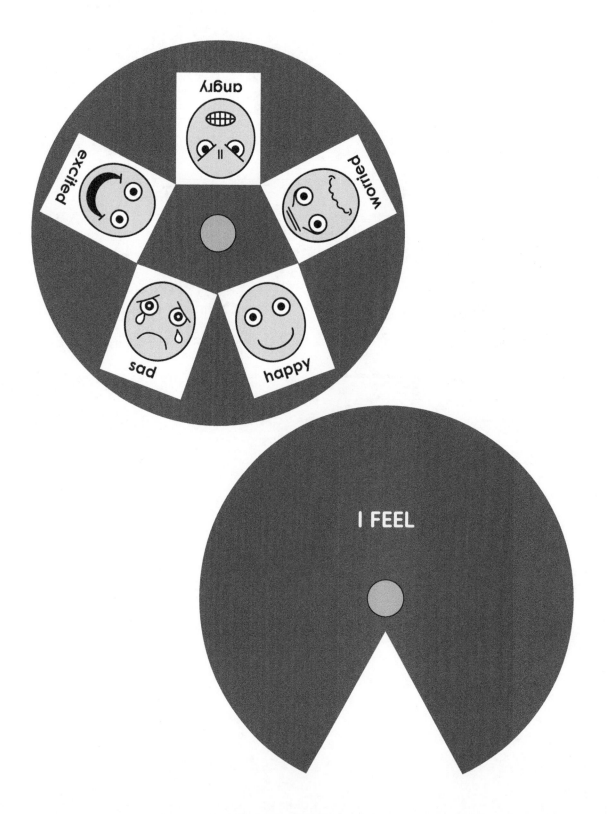

I feel

worried

Stick the large image onto a box and cut out the mouth shape.

Cut out the small cards below for children to write their worries on and post them into the 'Worry Box'.

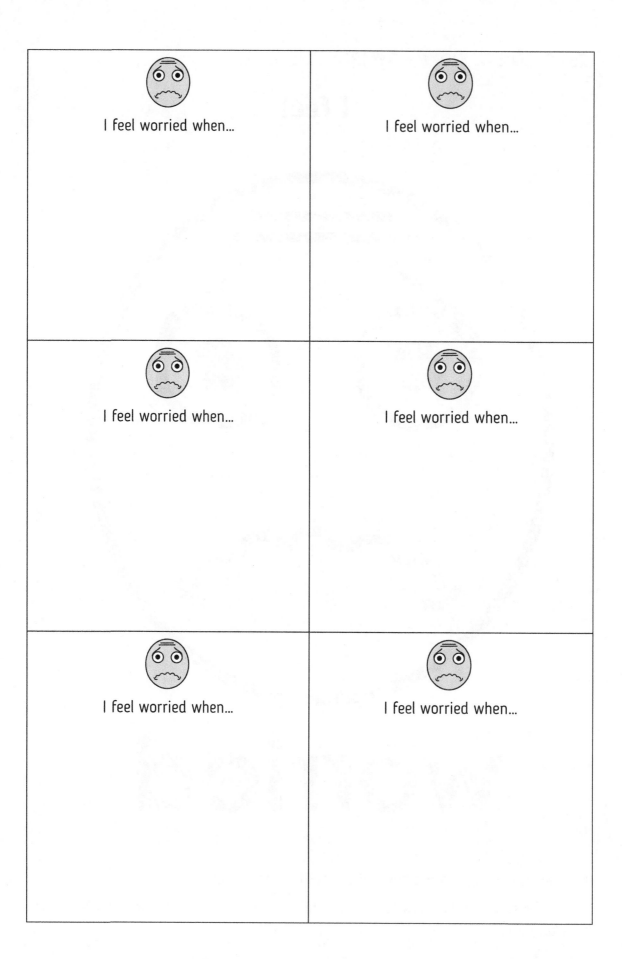

I feel worried when...

I feel worried when...

I feel worried when...

I feel worried when...

I feel worried when...

I feel worried when...

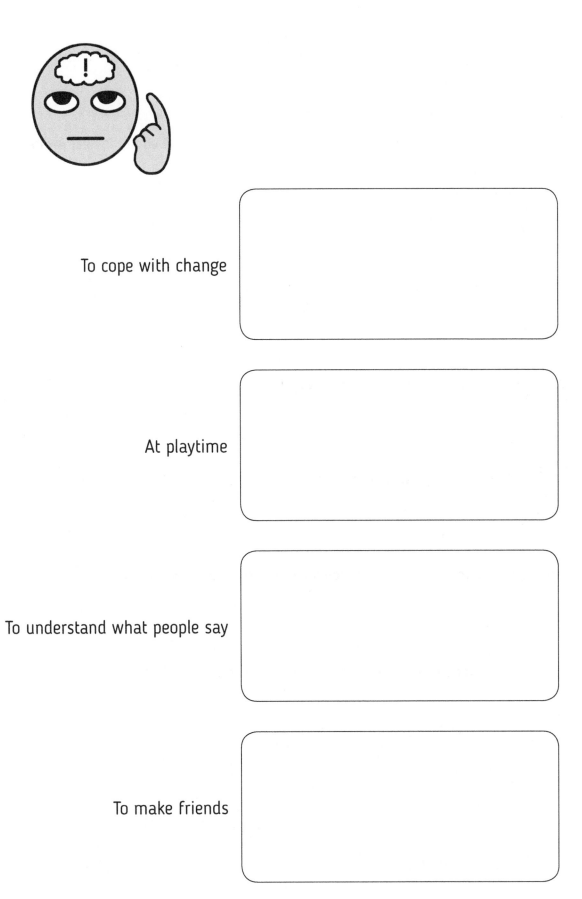

To cope with change

At playtime

To understand what people say

To make friends

14. PARENT RESOURCE: QUESTIONNAIRE FOR THE FAMILY

Name of child _____

Class _____   Date of meeting _____

When did your child receive a diagnosis? _____

Does your child know about their diagnosis?   **yes/ no**

Are you happy for your child to be asked if they wish to be involved in the Peer Awareness Assembly/Programme?   **yes/no**

Parents'/carers' views:

- What strengths and interests does your child have?

- What issues does your child have at school?

- What issues does your child have at home?

- How do you think your child could be supported by his/her peers?

- What information are you happy to be shared with your child's peers?

15. PUPIL RESOURCE: THINGS ABOUT ME I WOULD LIKE TO SHARE WITH MY CLASSMATES

THINGS ABOUT ME I WOULD LIKE TO SHARE WITH MY CLASSMATES		
ABOUT ME	Strengths and interests	Things I find difficult
THINGS I WOULD LIKE MY CLASSMATES TO HELP ME WITH		

SOCIAL COMMUNICATION

The pupil may take things literally and have difficulty understanding jokes and sarcasm. They may struggle to understand verbal and non-verbal communication, for example, gesture, facial expression, body language, and tone of voice.

I can help by:

SOCIAL RELATIONSHIPS

The pupil may find some social situations difficult to cope with and this could result in a particular behaviour to try to avoid a situation. Difficulty understanding social rules can lead to problems making and sustaining friendships.

I can help by:

STRENGTHS AND INTERESTS

SOCIAL IMAGINATION

The world often appears very unpredictable and the pupil finds comfort in routines they can control. They may become distressed over small changes in routines or the environment. The pupil may have difficulty predicting future events.

I can help by:

SENSORY

Many children may be hypersensitive to certain sensations or have low sensitivity. The pupil may need extra time to process sensory information and may not be able to filter sounds or prioritise what is important.

I can help by:

17. STAFF RESOURCE: HOW INCLUSIVE IS YOUR SCHOOL? QUESTIONNAIRE

Consider the following questions to evaluate how inclusive your school is for children with Autism. Ring the first circle if the statement is not achieved, the middle circle if partially achieved, and the final circle if achieved.

All staff have a raised awareness of Autism.	
All staff promote a positive attitude to difference.	
All staff have a commitment to including children with Autism in the life of the school.	
All staff have a commitment to partnership working with parents.	CHAMPIONS FOR AUTISM
All staff understand the importance of flexibility and are willing to change and adapt their provision to suit individual needs.	
The child with Autism has been involved in identifying strategies that would help them.	
Peers have a raised awareness of Autism.	
Peers are involved in assisting children with Autism to participate successfully in the life of the school.	

SOURCES OF INFORMATION

REFERENCES

Al-Ghani, K. I. (2008) *The Red Beast.* London: Jessica Kingsley Publishers.

American Psychiatric Association (2013) *Diagnostic and Statistical Manual of Mental Disorders, Fifth Edition (DSM-5).* Washington, DC: American Psychiatric Association.

Attwood, T. (2005) *The Complete Guide to Asperger's Syndrome.* London: Jessica Kingsley Publishers.

Baird, G., Simonoff, E., Pickles, A. Chandler, S. *et al.* (2006) *Prevalence of Disorders of the Autism Spectrum in a Population Cohort of Children in South Thames: The Special Needs and Autism Project (SNAP).* London: Elsevier.

Barnard, J., Prior, A. and Potter, D. (2000) *Inclusion and Autism: Is It working?* London: The National Autistic Society.

Baron-Cohen, S. and Bolton, P. (1993) *Autism: The Facts.* Oxford: Oxford University Press.

Bogdashina, O. (2003) *Sensory Perceptual Issues in Autism and Asperger Syndrome: Different Sensory Experiences, Different Perceptual Worlds.* London: Jessica Kingsley Publishers.

Carlin, J., Delamore, J. and Allard, A. (2014) *Dignity and Inclusion: Making it Work for Children with Behaviour that Challenges.* London: Council for Disabled Children.

Charman, T., Pellicano, L., Peacey, L. V., Peacey, N., Forward, K. and Dockrell, J. (2011) *What is Good Practice in Autism Education?* London: Centre for Research in Autism and Education (CRAE), Department of Psychology and Human Development, Institute of Education, University of London.

Department for Education and Skills (2004) *Removing Barriers to Achievement: Government Strategy for SEN.* London: Department for Education and Skills.

Department for Education and Department of Health (2015) *SEND Code of Practice: 0 to 25 Years, Statutory Guidance.* London: Department for Education.

Grandin, T. (1996) *Thinking in Pictures.* New York: Vintage Books.

Grandin, T. (2006) *Thinking in Pictures.* London: Bloomsbury Publishing.

Lawson, W. (2001) *Life Behind Glass.* London: Jessica Kingsley Publishers.

Montgomery, C. (1997) Quoted in 'A Unique Voice.' *Our Voice 3,* 1.

Morewood, G. D., Humphrey, N. and Symes, W. (2011) 'Mainstreaming autism: Making it work.' *GAP,* October 2011, 62–68.

National Autistic Society, The (2017a) 'Bullying and autism: Guidance for school staff.' Available at www.autism.org.uk/professionals/teachers/resource/bullying.aspx, accessed on 14/02/17.

National Autistic Society, The (2017b) 'A bullying guide for parents.' Available at www.autism.org.uk/about/in-education/bullying/guide-parents.aspx, accessed on 14/02/17.

Notbohm, E. (2007) *Ten Things Every Child with Autism Wishes You Knew.* Arlington, TX: Future Horizons.

Ochs, E., Kremer-Sadlik, T., Solomon, O. and Sirota, K. G. (2001) *Inclusion as Social Practice: Views of Children with Autism.* Oxford: Blackwell.

Powell, S. (2000) *Helping Children with Autism to Learn*, London: David Fulton Publishers.

Reid, B. and Batten, A. (2006) *B is for Bullied.* London: The National Autistic Society.

Shore, S. (2006) 'The Importance of Parents in the Success of People with Autism.' In C. Ariel and R. Naseef (eds) (2006) *Voices from the Spectrum.* London: Jessica Kingsley Publishers.

Stobart, A. (2009) *Bullying and Autism Spectrum Disorder.* London: Jessica Kingsley Publishers.

Warnock, H. M. (1978) *Report of the Committee of Enquiry into the Education of Handicapped Children and Young People.* London: Her Majesty's Stationary Office.

Wilkes, K. (2006) *The Sensory World of the Autistic Spectrum: A Greater Understanding.* London: The National Autistic Society.

World Health Organization (1992) *International Classification of Diseases and Related Health Problems (ICD-10).* Geneva: World Health Organization.

FURTHER READING

Al-Ghani, K. I. and Kenward, L. (2009) *Making the Move: A Guide for Schools and Parents on the Transfer of Pupils with ASD from Primary to Secondary School.* London: Jessica Kingsley Publishers.

Al Ghani, K. I. (2010) *Learning about Friendship.* London: Jessica Kingsley Publishers.

Baron Cohen, S. (2008) *Autism and Asperger Syndrome.* Oxford: Oxford University Press.

Batten, B., Corbett, C., Rosenblatt, M., Withers, L. and Yuille, R. (2006), *Make School Make Sense. Autism and Education: The Reality for Families Today.* London: The National Autistic Society.

Beaney, J. (2013) *Sensory Assessment and Intervention Programme.* London: Speechmark.

Beaney, J. and Kershaw, P. (2014) *Autism in the Primary Classroom.* London: The National Autistic Society.

Bondy, A. and Frost, R. (2011) *A Pictures Worth: PECS and other Visual Communication Strategies in Autism.* Bethesda, MD: Woodbine House Publishing.

Dublin, N. (2009) *Asperger Syndrome and Anxiety.* London: Jessica Kingsley Publishers.

Frith, U. (1994) *Autism, Explaining the Enigma.* Oxford: Blackwell Publishers.

Hannah, L. (2001) *Teaching Young Children with Autistic Spectrum Disorders to Learn.* London: The National Autistic Society.

Holzhauser-Peters, L. and True, I. (2009) *Making Sense of Children's Thinking and Behaviour.* London: Jessica Kingsley Publishers.

Gray, C. (1994) *Comic Strip Conversations.* New York: Future Horizons.

Gray, C. (2001) *My Social Stories Book.* London: Jessica Kingsley Publishers.

Kelly, A. (2011) *Talkabout for Children: Developing Social Skills.* London: Speechmark.

Larkey, S. (2007) *Practical Sensory Programmes for Students with Autistic Spectrum Disorder and other Special Needs,* London: Jessica Kingsley Publishers.

Seach, D. (2008) *Interactive Play for Children with Autism.* Abingdon: Routledge.

Sherratt, D. and Peter, M. (2002) *Developing Play and Drama in Children with Autism.* London: David Fulton.

Silver K. (2005) *Assessing and Developing Communication and Thinking Skills.* London: Jessica Kingsley Publishers.

Vermeulen, P. (2001) *Autistic Thinking: This is the Title.* London: Jessica Kingsley Publishers.

Wing, L. (2002) *The Autistic Spectrum.* London: Constable and Robinson.

USEFUL WEBSITES

The National Autistic Society

www.autism.org.uk

393 City Road
London
EC1V 1NG
020 7833 2299

The National Autistic Society produces some very useful leaflets and online resources on Autism and Asperger Syndrome. It also runs a helpline.

Autism Education Trust (AET)

www.autismeducationtrust.org.uk

c/o National Autistic Society
393 City Road
London
EC1V 1NG
020 7903 3650

The AET helps raise awareness of the importance of appropriate educational provision for children and young people on the Autism spectrum. The website has information about training opportunities, web-based resources and examples of good practice. There is a section on the website for children called 'Kids Zone', which contains information and games, and 'The Den', which is designed for teenagers.

CPI Antony Rowe
Eastbourne, UK
June 20, 2023